Robert Nelson

On the Epistle of James

Robert Nelson

On the Epistle of James

ISBN/EAN: 9783337729653

Printed in Europe, USA, Canada, Australia, Japan

Cover: Foto ©Thomas Meinert / pixelio.de

More available books at **www.hansebooks.com**

ON THE

EPISTLE OF JAMES.

BY

ROBERT NELSON,

AUTHOR OF "COMMENTS ON THE EPISTLE TO THE HEBREWS."

LONDON:
SAMUEL BAGSTER AND SONS,
15, PATERNOSTER ROW.
1872.

PREFACE.

In the Epistle of James, the student will doubtless have remarked the many sudden and abrupt changes of subject. Whereas in other epistles the argument flows on continuously until fully completed and the subject be exhausted, here there appears little or no connection in the sentences, which frequently follow one another without any noticeable relation. Very little arrangement is apparent in the topics—exhortation is the main feature; and this of so unusual a character, that the mind often feels at a loss to harmonise it with what is met with in other parts of the word of our God. And where instruction is given the discordance with other portions of the New Testament has been remarked, together with the difficulty of reconciling what is here put forth with the general teaching of the Scriptures. The footing upon which works are placed in the second chapter is a well-known instance of this. The definition of pure religion in chapter i. may also be adduced, and likewise the last verse of the epistle.

There is also to be noticed the absence of certain subjects to which it would be reasonable to expect that a prominent place would be assigned. The death of our Lord Jesus Christ is indeed alluded to in the expression, "Ye have condemned and killed the Just One"; but not a word is said about redemption by his blood.

Neither is the resurrection of our Lord so much as named; though the exhortation, " be patient unto the coming of the Lord," indicates that this most important subject was very far from being absent from the writer's thoughts.

Further, no mention is made of the pardon of sin through the efficacy of the one offering of Jesus! There must surely be some strong and peculiar motive for withholding this fundamental doctrine of the Christian faith, on the part of one who comes forward as " a servant of God, and of the Lord Jesus Christ."

Neither is Jesus spoken of anywhere in this epistle as Son of God. What can be the reason for this silence in James, one who had long been giving distinct testimony to this glorious fact? Moreover, the Holy Ghost is not even named; nor is eternal life mentioned; nor the oneness with Jesus; nor the sonship of the believer; nor his heirship; nor his future home in the heavens. In the present day were an enlightened Christian teacher to withhold these truths, it would be much commented on; and still more, were he to say nothing of the love of God in the gift of his Son, and of the love of the Son of God who loved us and gave himself for us.

Again, were a preacher of the gospel now to describe pure religion as comprehended in the two points, " visiting the fatherless and widows in their affliction," " and keeping himself unspotted from the world," would he not be considered to have very limited and imperfect views of divine revelation; passing over, as it does, all reference to love to God and to Christ, and even all notice of the Ten Commandments from Mount

Sinai? This verse cannot surely be a summary of the Sinaitic code, such as is given by our Lord in Matthew xxii. 37-40; nor can it be looked upon as containing, even in embryo, all the divine instruction for conduct, with which the epistles of Paul are filled.

It is not easy to discern any general scope or design in this epistle. From the omissions already noticed, it can scarcely be regarded as a preaching of the gospel. It is true that the "engrafted word" is named, as "able to save the soul"; and "the perfect law of liberty," under which phrase the gospel is apparently intended. But neither of these expressions, nor that of "the Lawgiver able to save," contains anything explicit as to the mode of the extension of mercy to the guilty, the helpless, and the lost. The epistle presents nothing of the nature of that sweet promise, "Believe on the Lord Jesus Christ, and thou shalt be saved."

Neither does it seem to be intended to instruct those who have so believed, and are consequently saved; since it does not present any of those high and glorious themes with which other epistles abound; intended to raise and animate the soul, teaching it to look forward to the glory that shall be revealed, encouraging it thereby to walk worthy of Jesus, who has called us unto his kingdom and glory.

A leading line of argument is not easily to be discovered. There are valuable instructions, detached and seemingly isolated, bearing some resemblance to the structure of the Book of Proverbs, rather than to any other part of the sacred writings.

Notwithstanding all these deficiencies, I do not see

the least reason to doubt the divine inspiration of this epistle. The Holy Ghost not only selects the persons through whom to send his messages, but also determines the purport of each message; so that the thoughts and the language in which they are clothed shall be exactly adapted to the state of mind and heart of those addressed.

For instance, it would not be judicious to address excited people in language suited to the quietude of an ordinary church-going population. Much more would this apply if the hearers were violently prejudiced against the speaker, and against the points he wished to introduce and commend to their notice. If he knew that they looked upon him as a renegade from their party, and viewed him with hatred, how much more cautious must he be in selecting suited thoughts, expressed in the briefest words, so as, if possible, to gain their attention. That James, on this occasion, under the control of the Holy Ghost, exercised such a wise and holy discretion, there is full reason to believe.

It seems not a little singular that this epistle should be regarded as addressed to the Christian Church. James himself declares that he writes to the Twelve Tribes. By what process of reasoning this designation is made to mean Christians, whether Jewish or Gentile, I am at a loss to discern. It is not even the two tribes of Judah and Benjamin, commonly called Jews, who are addressed. It is the whole of the tribes, the descendants of those whom God had brought out of Egypt by the hand of Moses. No Gentile could assert that the letter is written to him; though on taking it up, he may derive instruction from the perusal. If a letter were written to the Sandwich Islanders, it would not be proper for the people of Morocco to claim it as addressed to them; differing as they do both in nationality and in religion. The twelve tribes are not Christians. If any individual among them receive Jesus as the Christ, he at once ceases to belong to that nationality, because of the higher and nearer relationship to God into which he is thereby brought. He is now no longer a slave, but a free son; not as formerly, liable to ejection from the household; but, since the Son has made him free, he is permanently free. Israel, as we are taught in Galatians iv., was always a slave. It is only the Christian who is freeborn.

Those of the tribes of Israel who returned from the captivity in Babylon were not at all disposed to look upon the surrounding nations as one with themselves. They said to them (Ezra iv. 3), "Ye have nothing to do with us to build a house unto our God," etc. Nor would they, either in the time of our Lord, or now, admit Gentiles to claim that which exclusively belongs to themselves.

For a long period I saw no solution of the dislocated character of this epistle, nor of the apparent want of connected thought and argument. Some light at length dawned, on noticing that one subject, the government of the tongue, recurs again and again. It may be traced in chapters i. 19, 20, 26; ii. 7, 12; iii. throughout; iv. 11, 13; v. 9 (marginal reading), and 12. This led me to suspect that some undercurrent of thought pervaded the whole, though I could not then discern what it was.

It was, I think, the study of the seventh chapter of

the Acts which first gave me a clue. At one time that wonderful chapter seemed to me a mere recital of certain unconnected facts, without any bearing on one another, or on the momentous subject at issue. I now perceive them to be a series of events carefully selected and adjusted, so as to tell with cogent force upon the conscience of the people around. Stephen had been seized upon by violent hands, dragged immediately before a furious multitude, who were incensed against him, charged with a capital crime, without a moment to collect himself or arrange his thoughts. The same power that caused his face to shine as an angel gave him at once to pour forth an appeal so conclusive, so heart-stirring, that none of his adversaries could gainsay or resist it. As in similar cases, where the will is opposed to the convictions of conscience, they took refuge in violence. It was a marked instance of the fulfilment of that promise of our Lord: "But when they deliver you up, be not anxious how or what ye shall speak; for it is not ye that speak, but the Spirit of your Father that speaketh in you."

James now writes, not precisely to the same people, for those were inhabitants of Jerusalem, but to their kinsmen, the Twelve Tribes.

Further meditation has led me to an understanding of the consistency and wisdom of this portion of the counsel of God, which I now offer to my readers.

I do not enter upon the discussion whether James was one of the apostles. It is a point of small importance. Curiosity and research may be gratified by the inquiry; but I know of no spiritual benefit likely to arise by the fact being ascertained. Had any vital question depended upon it, we should no doubt have been clearly instructed upon the subject. The grand fact of the inspiration of the epistle must be judged of by the internal evidence. The early Church regarded it as inspired; and the stamp of inspiration is as distinct now as it was then. The gospels of Mark and Luke lose none of their importance by having been written by those who were not apostles. Nor is the inspiration of the Epistle to the Hebrews, or that of 1 John, to be questioned, though both are anonymous. Provided the communication be from God it is of no comparative moment to determine by what agent he may have been pleased to convey it. James does not declare himself to be an apostle; nor does Jude in his epistle, but it is most probable that both of them were of the twelve; since there were two brothers bearing those names, besides James, the brother of John, who was slain by Herod, as recorded in Acts xii. 2.

Malvern, 1872.

ON THE
EPISTLE OF JAMES.

CHAPTER I.

"James, a slave of God and of the Lord Jesus Christ, to the twelve tribes who are in the dispersion, greeting."

No disguise is used by James in commencing his address to his kinsmen according to the flesh. He boldly announces himself as belonging both to him whom the nation professes to worship, and to him whom they despise and reject, though he is indeed their rightful Sovereign. There was a double reason for describing himself as a slave. Not only was the clay moulded into human shape, kindled into life, and endowed with faculties and powers, but the very clay itself belonged to him who created it. Also, redemption price had been paid, by which also he had become the property of his Master. Both Paul, in Romans i. 1, and Peter (2 Pet. i. 1), speak of themselves as slaves of Jesus Christ. Another reason is found, in God having given them to Jesus, by virtue of which he has an additional title to them. The natural heart may shrink from this lowly and somewhat degrading appellation; yet those who know most of the grace of God and of his Christ, openly avow his title of absolute proprietorship over themselves; at the same time none knowing so well the glorious dignity to which they are exalted as Sons of God. In thus describing himself James likewise intimates the oneness of Jesus with God.

But neither does James, nor Peter, nor Paul hereby intimate that they considered themselves liable to a slave's rejection. On the contrary, the love of God in Christ admits of no rejection to those who come to him. At once they become heirs of God, and joint heirs with Christ. Nothing can separate us from his love. The full privilege of sonship is in no wise incompatible with the entire surrender of the will, the implicit obedience, so thoroughly displayed in Jesus, the beloved Son of God.

The letter is to the twelve tribes in the dispersion. The force of this word $\delta\iota\alpha\sigma\pi o\rho\grave{\alpha}$, "dispersion," may be traced in Deuteronomy iv. 27, xxx. 4, Isaiah xlix. 6, Ezekiel xii. 15; where it is seen to relate, not to any voluntary change of place, but to the forcible removal of Israel from their own land by the hands of their enemies. In 2 Kings xv. 29 we are told of Tiglath Pileser, king of Assyria, carrying away some of the tribes. Again, in 2 Kings xviii. 11, Shalmaneser, another king of Assyria, carried away the rest of the ten tribes. And in 2 Kings xxv. 11, the two remaining tribes, Judah and Benjamin, were transported to Babylon, from whence very few of them returned. Those spoken of in John vii. 35 seem rather to have been Jews residing in the Greek cities of Asia Minor. But all were looked upon with contempt by their highminded countrymen, being beyond the reach of the privileges of the land of Israel; therefore unclean and despicable. To these James now writes, accompanied with a friendly salutation. He does not call them saints, nor use any phrase equivalent to their having confessed Jesus as their Lord.

"My brethren, count it all joy when ye fall into various trials."

They were his brethren, children of the stock of Abraham. This term is also used by Stephen towards Jews, enemies of the Lord Jesus, in Acts vii. 1; and by Paul, in Acts xxii. 1 and xxiii. 1. Their common nationality is the basis of his address, from whence he can speak to them upon the miseries they are passing through. The denunciations, long threatened in Leviticus xxvi., had come upon them. Their position among the Gentiles was foretold to them in Deuteronomy iv. 27-30, and more fully in Deuteronomy xxviii. 25–48. In addition to all the fearful calamities therein described, and their being given over to idolatry, there are, in verse 65 of that chapter, these additional features of wretchedness:—"And among those nations shalt thou find no ease, neither shall the sole of thy foot have rest; but the Lord shall give thee a trembling heart, and failing of eyes, and sorrow of mind; and thy life shall hang in doubt before thee; and thou shalt fear day and night, and shalt have none assurance of thy life; in the morning thou shalt say, Would God it were even! and at even thou shalt say, Would God it were morning! for the fear of thine heart wherewith thou shalt fear, and for the sight of thine eyes which thou shalt see."

It is to these overwhelming trials James refers. Their most lamentable state of soul as regards God is described by the prophet Ezekiel xxxvii. 11 : "Behold, they say, Our bones are dried, and our hope is lost: we are cut off for our parts." Their hope in the God of their fathers being almost extinguished; persisting in the idolatry for which they were expatriated; given over to the corruptions which, in Romans i., are shown to be the consequence of the turning away from God; they yet reject the only means of obtaining light, life, and happiness, by refusing Jesus as the Christ. Under these circumstances, what can he say to comfort them? He knows it is the pleasure of their God, from Isaiah xl. 1, that they should be comforted. He would gladly lead them to the true source of consolation; but how shall he begin? To speak plainly would be to increase the hardening of their heart. We see in Jeremiah xlii. and xliv. what was the consequence of plain speaking to their forefathers when their minds were determined on pursuing a course of self-will. The obstinate nation, whose neck is an iron sinew, and the brow brass (Isa. xliv. 4), requires to be approached with more than common circumspection. They would neither be led nor driven. All the promises of their God they had learnt to disregard. His expostulations and endearing remonstrances they had despised. To his warnings and threatenings they took no heed. Visitations for sin sometimes induced compunction for a season, but without permanent effect. Now they had long been cast out from his presence. What fresh appeal shall be made so as, if possible, to affect their stony hearts? Sensitive, quick-witted, and intellectual, whatever is said must be pointed as well as brief. They will not bear much.

He begins then with their sorrows,—their widespread and overwhelming sorrows,—under the iron foot of the Gentile, by which they had long been trodden down. "Account it all joy," is the very singular commencement of his exhortation. Why should they account their trials to be joyous, in opposition to their daily experience? The brickmaking in Egypt had in it no vestige of joy. There their lives had been ground down with hard bondage, and they groaned under it. And the reason assigned for their accounting it all joy is not a little remarkable.

"Knowing that the testing your faith worketh endurance."

In order to pass an examination and merit approval, there must be effort. Effort necessitates endurance and strengthens it. So in all ages the exercise of faith demands endurance, as well as strengthens it. But to have endurance wrought in one is no special advantage further than in amending character on that point. The ascetic may practise it; so may the North American Indian. The labourer, the soldier, the sailor, all practise it constantly. But the benefit of such acquirement terminates with life. It reaches not beyond the grave. Here, however, the thing tested is faith, the faith of Israel.

In Romans v. 3-5 the apostle, speaking of tribulation, says that in the Christian it works endurance, and endurance experience (of God's favour), and experience hope, etc. It is not so said in this place. One of the special offices of the Comforter, whose descent among us was consequent upon the ascent of our Lord Jesus Christ, is to sustain the feeble faith of the Christian in the midst of his trials by pouring the love of God into his heart. But, in respect of the twelve tribes in the dispersion, the hope, as we have seen, was nearly lost.

Yet there was some faith in exercise. Possibly there may be an allusion to Leviticus xxvi. 40, where God was pleased to declare that, when pining away in their enemies' land, "if they shall confess their iniquity, and the iniquity of their fathers; if then their uncircumcised hearts be humbled, and they then accept the punishment of their iniquity: then I will remember my covenant with Jacob," etc. Whenever this takes place, the testing of their faith will meet with its reward; for then will God remember the land, and restore them to it.

But as far as regards the passage under consideration, nothing of this is expressed. The endurance is left without result. The whole horizon is blank and dark, save in one point where there is a gleam of light.

"But let the endurance have perfect work, that ye may be perfect and entire, lacking in nothing."

Could any amount of endurance accomplish this? Can it render a man perfect and entire, deficient in nothing? Were he to acquire all the endurance of Job himself, would he not be still a poor, miserable, lost sinner, destitute and helpless? Were he to build his hopes of perfection on such an attainment as this, it would be to imitate Adam in girding himself with fig leaves, insufficient to conceal his nakedness before God. No other means will avail than the reception of Jesus of Nazareth as God's one Remedy for all imperfection. United to him, the Son of God, by living faith, the sinner at once becomes perfect and entire, lacking in nothing. His blood cleanses the guilt; his righteousness furnishes admission into the presence of the Lord God Almighty: and in his life the one who trusts in him lives for ever. Unless endurance is allowed to accomplish the perfect work of bringing the sinner to the feet of Jesus, it leaves the whole undone. He is still a child of wrath, whatever his attainments may be. No one can be considered perfect before God until united to the Crucified One. James however, for the reasons already assigned, can only hint at this. Any one who so accepted Jesus would have a further burden to bear in the hatred of his brother Israelites. Their own Scriptures had, however, testified explicitly on the point: " We are all as an unclean thing, and all our righteousnesses as filthy rags." And again: Their righteousness is of me, saith the Lord. Also, Hosea x. 12: "It is time to seek the Lord, till he come and rain righteousness upon you."

" But if any of you lack wisdom, let him ask of God who gives (it) to all plainly, and upbraideth not, and it will be given him."

Here is apparently a very wide divergence of thought, an injunction to ask for wisdom, following immediately an exhortation to endure. In reality there is no divergence at all; but, on the contrary, a most intimate and gracious connection. For what purpose was this wisdom to be sought? Was it in regard to conduct of the general affairs of life, or for some specific object? The object, I apprehend, was specific, and the most momentous that could come before the mind of man. In John x. 24 the Jews came round Jesus and said to him, "How long dost thou make us to doubt? If thou be the Christ tell us plainly." They professed to doubt if he were the Christ! A little while before, John vii. 17, Jesus had said to them, "If any one wishes to do his (God's) desire, he shall know of the teaching whether it is from God, or whether I speak from myself." If the heart were sincerely desirous of learning whether Jesus of Nazareth were indeed the One of whom Moses in the law and the prophets had written, ample evidence had been already furnished, and more wisdom would be given to discern the facts. One Israelite "in whom was no guile" had already, in John i., been furnished with personal testimony. And in Luke xxiv. 45 the Lord opened the understanding of the eleven disciples that they might comprehend how the events they had seen explained the types, prophecies, and declarations of the Old Testament regarding the Messiah. To an Israelite it was the most vital of all questions whether Jesus was the Christ, for upon this his eternal happiness or misery depended. "Whosoever believes that Jesus is the Christ, is born of God." The God of all grace would not have his creature ignorant upon this all-important point. In attestation of Jesus being indeed the Christ, he supplied gifts of miraculous power in healing diseases, and in ability to speak many foreign languages by those who had never learned them.

Moreover, he does not upbraid those who seek him with their former hardness of heart, so as to put them to shame; nor does he refuse to impart the wisdom they now desire. The heart of our God is too tender to meet with a refusal him that comes to him.

"But let him ask in faith nothing hesitating. For he that hesitates is like a wave of the sea, driven with the wind and tossed. For let not that man think that he shall receive anything from the Lord."

To approach a monarch and ask for instructions, without intending to obey his command, would be to offer an insult to his majesty, which would justly bring down his wrath upon such an offender. How much more justly might wrath descend upon him who so mocks God! We read in Mark vi. 5 that Jesus in his own country could do no mighty work, because of their unbelief. His ability to work miracles there was as great as it was elsewhere, but the hardness of their hearts would have rendered fruitless such a display of divine power. Luke vi. 11 gives an instance of this. It is not the part of prudence to issue instructions where there is a moral certainty of their being resisted. "The fear of the Lord is the beginning of wisdom: and the knowledge of the holy is understanding." "This is his commandment, that we should believe on the name of his Son Jesus Christ" (1 John iii. 28). Unless the heart is willing to obey this command, it is useless to point out Jesus as the One to be obeyed. The children of Issachar (1 Chron. xii. 32), "who had understanding of the times, to know what Israel ought to do," were surely men who, using the language of the prophet, would say to their brethren, "O Israel, return unto the Lord thy God!"

"A double minded man is unstable in all his ways." As the varying wind drives now forward, now backward, the vessel exposed to its impulse, so the double minded or double souled man is unsteady in his course. " Ye cannot serve God and mammon" was the remark of our Lord. If the heart be given to God, it will seek to know his will in order to obey it. If this be not the case, the acquisition of divine knowledge produces no abiding benefit. On the contrary, the tendency is to steel the conscience and harden the heart.

" But let the brother of low degree rejoice in his elevation; but the rich in his humiliation, because as a flower of grass he will pass away. For the sun arose with its scorching wind, and the grass withered, and its flower drooped, and the comeliness of its appearance perished; so also will the rich man be dried up in his course."

What is the cause of the joy to the poor and to the rich man here referred to? It can scarcely be that the poor one should rejoice if raised to wealth and position, for then he would be exposed to the same dangers as the rich man. Nor can it be joy to the rich man to lose his property and position. The cause of joy is not here mentioned, though not difficult to be discovered. The cross of Jesus levels all earthly distinctions; it raises the beggar from the dunghill, and brings down the noble from his fancied greatness. He who trusts in Jesus, whether rich or poor, is exalted to reign in life with him in the heavens, in his Father's house. Yet, as regards earthly distinction, each must be prepared to be ranked with him who, while here, was despised by the people, and without a place to lay his head. In the land of Israel, the vegetation may be green and flourishing one day; the next day withered and dried up through the setting in of the burning wind. Isaiah also dwells upon the same point, chapter xl., as further enforced by Peter. God's remedy for this is the gospel of his dear Son (1 Pet. i. 25).

"Happy the man who endures trial; for, when approved, he will receive the crown of life which the Lord promised to them who love him."

Happy indeed is he who not merely bears affliction with fortitude, for this will in no way contribute to the salvation of his soul, but he who, recognising the purpose for which it is sent, is thereby drawn near to God; brought out of a state of enmity into fellowship with him. Through Jesus alone this can be accomplished; in him alone can the sinner be approved. Union with him kindles in the heart love to God. The crown of life is the glorious portion of all who receive Jesus: "he who hath the Son hath the life, and he who hath not the Son of God hath not the life." "Eye hath not seen, nor ear heard, neither hath it entered into the heart of man the things that God hath prepared for those who love him." (Isaiah lxiv. 4, as cited in 1 Corinthians ii. 9.)

"Let no one, being tempted, say that, 'I am tempted from God': for God cannot be tempted with evil (things); neither tempteth he any one. But each is tempted by his own desires, drawn out, and caught by a bait. Then desire having conceived brings forth sin. But the sin being accomplished brings forth death."

Nothing is more common in the heart of man than to charge God with its own crimes. Adam did this when he said, "The woman that thou gavest me, she gave me of the tree, and I did eat." Ever insisting on its own innate goodness, it is prone to assert, "If I had not been endowed with these propensities; if temptation had not been placed in my way, I should have conducted myself with propriety." That is, if man had been formed without the beneficial endowments which God has bestowed upon him, and if this world had contained no object of attraction to him, he would have remained upright. But of which of his faculties or powers would he consent to be destitute? and would he be content were there no objects of gratification? He would not be pleased were this earth a wilderness, and himself a stone! Neither would such a state of things comport with the magnificent designs of his Creator towards him.

In Jeremiah vii. 8 the Lord God, expostulating with Israel, says, Behold ye trust in lying words that cannot profit. Will ye steal, murder, and commit adultery, and swear falsely, and burn incense unto Baal, and walk after other gods whom ye know not; and come and stand before me in this house, which is called by my name, and say, We are delivered to do all these abominations? Their plea was a false plea: they had at Sinai been forbidden to do these things, and there was no justification.

"God cannot be tempted with evil (things)." Saul tried this. He brought the best of the sheep and oxen (1 Sam. xv. 15), which should have been utterly destroyed, to sacrifice unto the Lord. Another motive was found in this, as in all such cases, lurking beneath. It is only too common to profess to honour God by doing that which he has forbidden.

But James would perhaps be intending that the principle just laid down should operate in this way. The whole nation, led on by its rulers, priests, and elders, had rejected Jesus as the Messiah, notwithstanding all the evidence furnished as to his title. What could the scattered ones do but accept their decision? They might allege that they were not so learned as the others; that they were not on the spot to form a personal judgment on the events; and that proper deference to the heads of the nation required them to adopt their sentiments. The latent motive for all this would be the fear of man, setting aside the fear of God. But there was yet a motive deeper than this: the rebellion of their own hearts against their God and his commands. The sin of rejecting Jesus can only issue in eternal death.

"Be not misled, my beloved brethren. All good giving, and every perfect gift, is from above, coming down from the Father of the lights, with whom there is not any variation or turning shade. Of his own will he brought us forth by a true word, that we should be a certain firstfruits of his creatures."

We read in John i. that "the law was given by Moses." He was from the earth, earthy. And though in itself the law was holy, just, and good, yet, through the inability of man to keep it, the desired end was not attained. The hope of life receded, the prospect of acquiring it constantly diminished. Moreover their God, speaking in Ezekiel xx. 25, said, "Wherefore I gave them also statutes that were not good, and judgments whereby they should not live." But they persisted in holding tenaciously by these notwithstanding, though making little effort to obey. So that, when grace and truth came to them from heaven in the person of Jesus, they refused both him and them. Yet he was the perfect Gift, so freely bestowed by the Father, from whom alone real bounty emanates; he, in his largeness of heart, bestowing the greatest of his treasures on the most worthless of his creatures. It was by him that the sun and the moon were formed and appointed to diffuse light and warmth even upon the unthankful and the evil. The sun, however, descends below the horizon, and the moon during a period is invisible. Darkness supervenes. Yet he who called Israel by name, and separated them from the nations to be his own peculiar people, his inheritance, he, their God, neither slumbereth nor sleepeth. He was also pleased to declare (Mal. iii. 6), "For I, the Lord, change not, therefore ye sons of Jacob are not consumed." He has acknowledged them as his firstborn, (Exod. iv. 22), and likewise as the firstfruits of his increase (Jer. ii. 3). To these blessed assurances of perpetual favour, and of the fountain from whence it flows, James now seeks to draw the attention of the dispersed nation. The psalmist speaks of many saying, "Who will show us good?" and replies, "Lord, lift thou up the light of thy countenance upon us!" Its benignity infuses joy into the heart!

Though Israel was thus the firstfruits of God's increase, having the dignified position of firstborn among the nations, yet is there another, a far more glorious Firstfruits,—the Lord Jesus Christ himself; the Firstfruits of those who have slept; the First-begotten from the dead. He is the Firstfruits of the resurrection family, of those who live for ever; and we who trust in him, as one with him, become firstfruits unto God.

"So that, my beloved brethren, let every man be swift to hear, slow to speak, slow to wrath; for the wrath of man worketh not the righteousness of God."

From the combination of so many injunctions in this passage, coupled with the intimation that righteousness is not to be attained by giving way to wrath, it is evident that something is alluded to beyond what meets the eye. It cannot surely be that James is inculcating an eagerness to hear new things, such as pervaded the Athenians in Acts xvii. 21. Nor would it be mere restraint of utterance, nor self-control as to anger, which, though worthy of constant attention, would not appear in any way connected with the righteousness of God. The sequence would seem to convey that they are to be actively desirous of listening to something which is not specified, slow to speak in opposition to it, and carefully to avoid anger in respect to it; for such anger will not be of any account towards obtaining such righteousness as God can approve of. What can it be that they are unwilling to hear, ready to oppose, and apt to lose temper about, so as to impede the attainment of the righteousness of God?

The solution is, I think, to be found in verse 18, where the true word is mentioned, whereby Israel was constituted God's peculiar people (Deut. xiv. 2). The very same word had also spoken of One who was to be their Ruler, their Saviour, their Deliverer; who was to save his people from their sins, by bearing them in his own person; who was to be the despised and rejected of men, and against whom the kings of the earth set themselves, and the rulers took counsel together : even against him, the anointed King and Priest,—against the Father as well as against his Son. That they had done all this in their conduct towards Jesus of Nazareth was fully proved by all the testimonials recorded in Matthew xxvii. ; by God having raised him from the dead ; and by the descent of the Holy Ghost; through whom the poor ignorant fishermen and others, who had followed him while on earth, were able, to their own astonishment, to work miracles in his name, to prophesy and speak languages they had never learned.

But to all this the nation, with its characteristic obstinacy, was very unwilling to listen, though accompanied with a fresh offer of mercy, remission of sins, and acceptance, if they would now acknowledge him as the Christ of God. The word by which they were to be comforted, so long before promised them through Isaiah, they are now told is the very word which, by the gospel, is preached unto them. If they refuse this source of comfort, they deprive themselves of all comfort; for there is none other name under heaven given among men whereby they can be saved! James now endearingly asks them to listen to this good news, to give it a patient hearing, to reflect upon it, by no means to indulge in the outburst of wrath against Jesus, so common among their countrymen, to execrate whom had become in their eyes a token of zeal for God. To call Jesus anathema (accursed) (1 Cor. xii. 2), could in no way be pleasing to God, and in no way conduce to their attainment of righteousness ; but, on the contrary, would directly obstruct their obtaining it, themselves shutting the door in their own faces.

"Wherefore, putting away all filthiness and abundance of malice, in meekness receive the implanted Word, who is able to save your souls."

The malice against the person of Jesus found its expression in the mode which travellers assure us is customary with orientals. Job iii. furnishes a specimen of this; and Jeremiah xx. 14. Both these, however, are comparatively free from the gross indecency, though giving way to the abounding malice here mentioned. Possibly, Peter's denial, as given in Mark xiv. 71, was of this character. Putting away all this, receive him whom you have hitherto rejected, despised, and insulted, who alone is able to save your souls. It is sometimes difficult to trace the transition from the written word to Him who is emphatically The Word, through whom God has spoken in these last days. Whether the written word is intended in this passage, or the Lord himself, as seems probable, the purport would be nearly identical, since the writings of the Old Testament are full of the person of the blessed Son of God. Receive him, and you are at once made partaker of the promises announced in John i. 12, and of all the promises which God has treasured up in Christ for those who receive him. Therefore, renounce all the hard thoughts you have hitherto entertained, and now welcome him with meekness as the precious gift of God.

This verse conveys a plain indication of the state of soul of those addressed. They were not at that time in the condition of saved persons. They had not yet received the implanted word. They still continued in their malignity against Jesus, giving utterance to it in vile and gratuitous insult, such as their nation has continued to use. They are exhorted to cease from all this, and receive him who can save them from the coming wrath. Paul has a corresponding desire and prayer in Romans x. 1, when he says, " Brethren, my heart's desire and prayer to God for Israel is, that they may be saved."

The expression, " implanted Word," cannot relate to being implanted in the heart, since this had not been done. It may allude to the declaration in Psalm i. 3 : " He shall be like a tree planted by the rivers of water :" a passage clearly relating to our Lord. Also to Psalm xcii. 12, 13—the Palm-tree and the Cedar planted in the house of the Lord—Himself the most eminent of all. In Romans vi. 5, there is an expression somewhat similar : " If we have been planted together (with him) in the likeness of his death, we shall be also in that of the resurrection." All these three passages seem to convey that Jesus is already planted in resurrection, where he dwells supreme in the house of the Lord for ever, prospering in whatever he undertakes. Blessed be his name!

" But become doers of the word, and not hearers only, deceiving yourselves. For if any one is a hearer only, and not a doer of the word, this (person) is like a man beholding his natural face in a mirror : for he beholds himself, and goes, and immediately forgets what he was. But whosoever stoops * unto the perfect law, that of freedom, and continues, this person not becoming a forgetful hearer, but a doer of the word, he will be happy in that which he does."

---

* παρακύπτω to stoop down. See John xx. 5 and 11.

To do what that word enjoins, that is, to believe in Jesus, is to become a possessor of eternal life. Otherwise, the mere knowledge how salvation is to be obtained, only adds to the condemnation. The self-deception of Christendom is appalling. Avowing universally that faith in Christ is essential, how small a proportion ever come to him, listen to his voice, or obey him!

As in the case of a man looking at himself in a mirror, while he continues to look he beholds his own features, but forgets them when he turns away; so he who contemplates himself as reflected by the gospel, perceives that by nature he is helpless and undone, yet, by the grace of God, capable of being brought out of the ruin by owning Jesus as his Master, and trusting in him. Having ascertained this, if he then turns away, he falls back upon his own estimate of himself, not by any means so disparaging, though deceptive and false.

But he who does stoop from his high notion of himself unto the law of freedom, and continues, without turning back, as some of the disciples did, in John vi. 66, he will be happy eternally; and this act of his will be the instrumental cause of his happiness. To the Israelite mind this was indeed a degradation. To place himself on the same footing as the Gentile, expecting salvation on the same terms; to give up his own righteousness and be indebted to another for it and for the consequent hope of life; and, still worse, to look to one crucified for these things, would be a great lowering of himself in his own eyes and those of his associates.

The idea of "doing work," here introduced, probably alludes to the predominant thought in the mind of

Israel, "What shall I do to inherit eternal life?" "This do, and thou shalt live." The thought is more fully dwelt upon in the next chapter.

"The law of freedom" is a phrase which could only be comprehended by one in the circumstances and frame of mind of an Israelite. We are told in Galatians iv. 24, that the covenant from mount Sinai gendereth to slavery. It was, in allegory, the Hagar covenant; and, Hagar, being a slave-woman, her children, though begotten of Abraham, were slave-children. The Christian alone is the free man. To this the apostle alludes in Romans viii. 15, "For ye have not received the spirit of slavery again to fear," etc. The slave's position and the slave's spirit alike pertained to Israel. The demand on them, and, on their part, the desire and the effort was to do what might insure to them eternal life: a permanent demand, and a ceaseless, life-long labour, compared with which, to the awakened conscience, the task-work in Egypt was but the play of childhood: a yoke, said Peter, which neither our fathers nor we were able to bear. Contrasted with this is the law of freedom. On receiving Christ the slave's fetters are struck off. Through union with him he becomes a free man. He is delivered from the requirements and the penalties of the law of Moses, and is welcomed by Jesus as one whom his Father has given him: his own property, never to be parted with.

Law work produces no happiness. There was a ceaseless round of obligation never fulfilled, and, consequently, a bad conscience, with its attendant miseries. Nothing but the blood of Jesus can give it ease. When it becomes known to the soul of the sinner that the Master has paid the demand against him in his own life's blood, his anxiety ceases, and he is at peace.

"If any one thinks [δοκεῖ] (or seems) to be religious, not bridling his tongue, but deceiving his heart, the religion of this (person) is vain."

Whether the thought be that the man thinks himself religious; intends to be so; is accounted religious by others; or that he merely pretends to be so (for all these ideas seem capable of being contained in the Greek word); in all these cases his religion is vain if he bridles not his tongue. The declaration is very strange, and, if it stood alone, perfectly inexplicable. Many godly men are unhappily not always found to bridle their tongues, and whose pens are at times dipped in gall; yet we dare not refuse them the rank and position of a Christian if sufficient evidence otherwise exists of their Christianity. As with every other sin committed by a Christian, we should greatly deplore this sin, and feel that he has thereby dishonoured his Lord and disgraced himself. But were we to say that bursts of temper exclude a man from salvation, it would be tantamount to asserting that it is by good conduct we are saved, and not by the death and life of Jesus. Yet, in the connection in which this passage stands, it is perfectly and absolutely true. Unless the tongue be bridled when it speaks of Jesus, if it still gives utterance to those familiar words of execration in which the Jewish heart has long indulged itself, vain is all pretence of religion. The Lord said while he was on earth, "He that honoureth not the Son honoureth not the Father who hath sent him." Vain therefore is the religion of him who refuses Jesus! refusing, as he does, the only means by which his person or his service can become acceptable to God. It was the most religious part of the nation which made the conspiracy to murder the Son of God. On religious grounds the sanhedrim condemned him. The insult they heaped on the Holy One, while on the cross, was all religious. Surely, if men ever deceived their own hearts, and stamped vanity upon their own religiousness, it was on this occasion. And so must it ever be with those who follow in the same path.

"This is clean* religion, and undefiled with God and the Father, To watch over orphans and widows in their affliction; to keep himself unspotted from the world."

Perhaps this verse excites more astonishment than any in the epistle. Were any one in our day to present this as an epitome of religion, great would be the outcry throughout the land. Would it not be said, " Here is a definition of religion in which neither Christ nor God are presented? a religion which neither recognises man's ruin, nor God's grace; a religion of which good works are the basis and substance, and comprising two only out of the multitude of moral obligations incumbent upon man; a religion without a centre and without a hope, which cannot be called the Christian religion since it speaks not of faith in Christ; neither can it be called the faith of Israel, since it ignores the first table of the commandments, and scarcely finds a standing-place in the second table, the greater part of which is left entirely out of sight. It cannot be said to comprise either the law or the prophets, much less the commands of Christ and his apostles.

* Not ἁγνός pure, but καθαρὸς, from καθαίρω, to cleanse.

Is it not evident that James, the servant of Christ, who long listened to the truths his Master taught, and had since been teaching them to others; who had seen his Master expire on the cross on account of the sins of his people; and who was one of those announcing salvation to Israel through a risen Saviour, for whose sake he had renounced the faith in which he had been brought up; is it not evident that he could not be intending by these words to define either the Christian or the Jewish religion, seeing it presents neither one nor the other?

What then can be his intention? We have seen that he is addressing the Twelve Tribes. Further, from verse 21, that they had not embraced the gospel, and were as yet unsaved. Also, that they were full of hatred against the Lord Jesus Christ; on which account he could say very little to them of all that lay upon his heart to say. Moreover, that they were in the dispersion. This last point involves much that was incidental. In the first place, they were away from the land of Israel, and consequently away from the temple; if indeed it still existed at the date of the epistle. They could therefore carry out none of the prescribed observances; they could neither offer burnt-offerings, peace-offerings, nor sin-offerings. The holy feasts they could not attend. The Passover, if practised by them, was nothing but an empty form, since they were far away from the spot where their God had been pleased to place his name; where alone, in his presence, the feast could be celebrated. The day of atonement furnished no comfort to them. They could not share in its solemnities, and could not tell whether they were observed or not. The various cleansings required by the law could not be performed, since God's altar was far off from them, and they were consequently in a state of perpetual ceremonial defilement. True it was, they had synagogues, but these were not places for worship; they were merely buildings for reading and expounding the law. The temple, where God dwelt, was the only place where to approach his presence, and offer him an oblation or worship.

In addition to their spiritual ruin, we perceive, in chapters 4 and 5, their grievous state of demoralization.

Under all these circumstances what could James say to them? He could not re-inforce the Law, since it was impossible to observe it; besides, the time for its observance had come to an end, in consequence of Christ having come (Gal. iii. 19). To the gospel they would not listen. He can only speak on such points as remain within the range of their moral consciousness, no religious observances being practicable. But widows and orphans are found among them. These may be looked after. It had not been their habit so to do. Isaiah i. 23, says, "They judge not the fatherless, neither doth the cause of the widow come unto them." Jeremiah v. 3, testifies to the same effect. The last of the prophets, Malachi iii. 5, declares that God will specially notice such oppression. Nevertheless, from Matthew xxiii. 14, it would seem that the scribe and Pharisee paid little attention to the prohibition or the threatening. Perhaps the heart of those in the dispersion may be more susceptible, being themselves in misery. If they can do nothing more, they may attend to this, which is within their reach; and it may yet be the means of restoring the soul, should they find themselves so far concurring with him who has declared himself to be "a Father of the fatherless, and a Judge of the widows" (Ps. lxviii. 5).

Where all was in hopeless ceremonial defilement, here, at least, is a fragment of the divine mind; a small portion of religious duty which in itself is not unclean. According to Haggai ii. 14, the Jews then engaged in rebuilding the temple, being themselves unclean, defiled everything they touched. Yet was their work both commanded by God, and accepted by him; and themselves were blessed in consequence of obeying his orders. That is to say, their fields were no longer barren, nor their trees unproductive; nor did their grain waste away in the granary, though the yoke of the Gentile was not removed from their necks.

In a similar point of view may the other definition be regarded: "to keep himself unspotted from the world." In the higher Christian sense, as the rejecters of Jesus, this could not possibly apply. Neither, as we have seen, could it be intended in the legal and ceremonial sense, in which Israel as a nation were required to walk as God's peculiar people in separation from the Gentile world; for their present circumstances no longer admitted of this. Long before their God said regarding them: "I have forsaken mine house, I have left mine heritage, I have given the dearly beloved of my soul into the hands of her enemies." Yet in their dispersion they might still refrain from the evil principles and practices of the scribes and Pharisees condemned in Matthew xxiii.; and from those abominations noted in Leviticus xviii. 19, 20, practised by the Gentiles, and by themselves also, against which the Lord set his face; and on account of which he had threatened to cast them out, as he cast out the nations before them. Nevertheless, after they had been scattered among the Gentiles, they still profaned the name of the Lord, and by their wickedness caused it to be blasphemed (Ezek. xxxvi. 20; Rom. ii. 24). Their state of alarm and distress of mind while in their enemies' land is described beforehand in Leviticus xxvi. 36, 37, as well as in Deuteronomy xxviii. 65–67. The hope of some alleviation might, as in the case of Nebuchadnezzar (Dan. iv. 27), and in accordance with the promise in Proverbs xxviii. 13, induce in them some attention to what James is here presenting.

———o———

CHAPTER II.

"My brethren, do not have the faith of the glorious Lord Jesus Christ with respect of persons. For if there enter into your synagogue a man with a gold ring, in gay clothing; and a poor man also come in a dirty dress, and ye should look upon him wearing the gay clothes, and say to him, Sit thou here in a good place; and to the poor one you should say, Stand thou there, or sit here under my footstool, would you not make differences among yourselves, and become judges of evil considerations?"

The argument here, I apprehend, instead of identifying as Christians those addressed, does in reality disprove such an opinion. If the word translated "assembly" were rightly so rendered, the point might be questioned;

but it is everywhere else, with only one exception out of fifty-seven places, translated "synagogue." James does not assert that they have the Christian faith. His admonition is against coupling respect of persons with the Christian faith. And he appeals to practices in the synagogues, where such partiality is particularly to be noticed: the well-dressed person being placed in a conspicuous seat, while the poor man is scarcely allowed to sit at all, or only on the ground under the feet of the more respectable class. The stress of this remonstrance is, not in favour of Christianity, but against synagogue usages; the impropriety of which, in this particular, the apostle points out subsequently. True it is he speaks hypothetically, but it is evident from what follows that the picture is not ideal. And it is not a little singular how, in so-called Christian assemblies, the same principle prevails, and is without scruple maintained. James, as the servant of God and also of Christ, could say no less than that such practices were at variance with both the Christian and the Israelite faith. And it is only in this incidental way that he can venture to name distinctly the faith of Christ, only by alluding to its discordance with behaviour such as this, which their own judgment also would perceive to be at variance with what their Scriptures directed. He now proceeds to expound the Mosaic law, not the gospel of the grace of God in Christ.

"Hearken, my beloved brethren, Has not God chosen the poor of the world, rich in faith, and heirs of the kingdom which he promised to those that love him?"

From the mention of "the kingdom," we at once judge it to mean the kingdom that cannot be shaken, for which the Christian is entitled to look with joyful expectation. But is there not also another kingdom spoken of in the Scriptures, announced by the prophet (Zech. ix. 9), "Rejoice greatly, O daughter of Zion! shout, O daughter of Jerusalem! Behold! thy King cometh unto thee:" an appeal responded to by the multitudes as Jesus entered his own royal city of Jerusalem, when they shouted, "Hosanna! blessed is he who comes in the name of the Lord! Blessed be the kingdom of our father David, that comes in the name of the Lord! Hosanna in the highest!" It was this kingdom on which the heart of Israel was fixed. Nationally they knew of no other. It had long been specifically and repeatedly promised to them by God, and for this they were waiting. They were nationally the children of the kingdom (Matt. viii. 12). Theirs was the children's bread, not intended for the dogs, the Gentiles. For those among them who love God is this kingdom still kept, though so long in abeyance. All of them were heirs of this kingdom, inasmuch as they were of the seed of Abraham according to the flesh, which God had set apart for himself. But only the faithful ones eventually obtain. The unbelievers will be rooted out. Those among them who receive Jesus as the Christ before he comes forth in his glory, become heirs of the far higher glory and kingdom in the heavens, when he sits at the right hand of God.

To both these kingdoms the poor as well as the rich are admitted on the same terms. There is no partiality. The poor Israelite was as much an heir as the rich Israelite. The birthright gave the title. To the still higher dignity, and the everlasting life, all, whether rich or poor, are equally welcomed. "The same Lord over all is rich unto all who call upon him." But herein is God's procedure totally diverse from that of man. No earthly monarch, possessed of unlimited authority, was ever known to favour all his subjects equally. He has honours and rewards for the nobles which the poor cannot hope to share. But when God selects, he takes the poor, degraded, debased, heart-broken Egyptian slave, and exalts him above his fellow-men as heir of the one kingdom; and the poor beggars and outcasts of society are sought for in the highways and under the hedges, and invited to come and be made heirs of God, joint heirs with Christ.

"But ye have despised the poor [one]. Do not the rich [ones] oppress you? and they drag you before judgment seats. Do not they blaspheme the good name which is called upon you?"

You have, as has been shown, disallowed the claim of the poor, and treated him with contumely. But there was One, the poorest of the poor, not having where to lay his head: how have you all treated him? He grew up as a root out of dry ground, a Man of sorrows, oppressed, afflicted, brought as a lamb to the slaughter, cut off out of the land of the living! Call to mind that the Lord laid upon him the iniquity of us all! Have you no fellow-feeling for him, your brother in affliction? Somewhat to this effect perhaps might the expostulation have proceeded had it been practicable.

The rich people here mentioned seem of a different class from those in chapter v. 1. Here they appear to be Gentiles, their rulers and oppressors, who likewise blaspheme the name of the God of Israel. In

Isaiah lxiii. 19, Israel is made to say to God, respecting the Gentiles, "Thou never bearest rule over them: they were not called by thy name." On the other hand in Jeremiah xiv. 9, Israel says, "We are called by thy name." And Daniel ix. 19 speaks of the city and people called by the name of God. Psalm lxxiv. 18 and lii. 5 tell of Gentiles blaspheming the name of Israel's God. Have you not reason therefore to mistrust the possession of wealth instead of boasting in it?

"If ye fulfil the royal law according to the scripture, Thou shalt love thy neighbour as thyself, ye do well: but if ye have respect of persons, ye commit sin, and are convicted by the law as transgressors."

The royal law commanded each Israelite to love his neighbour as himself. The neighbour is specially mentioned, so many causes of irritation and ill-will arising among those who reside in close proximity. The injunction does not extend to their conduct towards foreign nations, some of whom were to be slain, others reduced to slavery, and some, Moab and Ammon, to be forever excluded from fellowship. This portion was not the whole of the royal law. It was the substance of the second table; not of the first, the great commandment. It was well to conform so far, though it left untouched the greater injunction, "Thou shalt love the Lord thy God with all thine heart, and with all thy soul, and with all thy strength" (Deut. vi. 5; Matt. xxii. 27).

The law of Moses is here seen to search the heart, and discriminate in a way one is little prepared to expect. Carelessness as to whether the man in dirty clothing sits or stands, or the assigning him a degrading seat, while the well-dressed man is respectfully treated, criminates the one who so acts as guilty before God. He is a sinner, a transgressor of the royal law. It shows respect to garments, not to the neighbour; disrespect to the neighbour because of garments; in both cases there is a setting aside of God's law, because of man's preferences. This is an indignity to the King of kings.

"For whoever shall keep the whole law, but stumble in one [point] he is guilty of all. For he who said, Do not commit adultery, said also, Do not kill. But if thou dost not commit adultery, but killest, thou art become a transgressor of law."

The law of God given through Moses was one law, one code. It contained a multitude of precepts and prohibitions, which men divide into moral and ceremonial. Theoretically they may be so discriminated, but no such distinction was allowed in practice. Moses, in Leviticus xviii. 5, speaking of God's statutes and judgments, says, "which, if a man do, he shall live in them." Paul, in Romans x. 5, writing of the law, repeats the same promise. And our Lord, in Matthew v. 18, 19, describes the whole as one. Therefore the transgression of one enactment brought the individual under sentence of death, as guilty. Whilst in another point of view, it deprived him of all hope of life since he had failed to keep the whole law, on the entire fulfilment of which his life depended. Man is very apt to set off, as regards himself, one good deed against another bad one; to justify himself in one guilty act by alleging righteous conduct on another point. Here all such ground is taken away from under his feet.

And thus does James plainly show to his brethren,

through the little, familiar habit in the synagogue, that their supposed righteousness crumbles away to nothing, and that they really are naked and destitute before God.

"So speak ye and so act as about to be judged by freedom's law. For to him that has not acted with mercy there is merciless judgment. Mercy exults over judgment."

Having brought them up to this point, he again introduces the remedy, the only remedy—the law of freedom, or rather freedom's law. Slave law, already brought to their notice in chapter i. 25, entails, as he has shown, guilt and death, furnishing no hope of life. And, however fondly and tenaciously they might cling to it, the futility was too apparent. Happily for them and for us sinners universally, God had made another provision, adequate to the emergency, the law of the Spirit of life in Christ Jesus. To this glorious arrangement of mercy they are again exhorted to submit themselves. He cannot speak of it in plain terms because of the hardness of their hearts; but he presents it now in a touching aspect.

They, as a nation, had shown no mercy to their own Brother! In his misery they had insulted and disowned him, demanding his crucifixion. When the judge remonstrated, "Why, what evil hath he done?" their only reply was, still louder and more fierce demands for his death, in this most ignominious and agonising form. Not one of all the multitudes he had healed came forward to attest his divine power, or his kindness. Not one of those whose hearts he had comforted by restoring husband, son, or brother to health and strength, made any appeal in his behalf. They knew him to be innocent, yet plotted to destroy him. Rather than release him, they imprecated the guilt of shedding his blood upon themselves and upon their children. Truly they had shown no mercy to the Son of God, and by righteous retribution they could expect no mercy. God's command was, "Thou shalt take no satisfaction for the life of a murderer" (Num. xxxv. 31); and "thou shalt take him from mine altar, that he may die" (Exod. xxi. 14). Such and no less was the penalty that awaited them as the guilty murderers of God's Son.

But in the heart of their God mercy exulted over judgment. Long before he had been pleased to say by the mouth of his servant Ezekiel, xxxiii. 11, "As I live, saith the Lord God, I have no pleasure in the death of the wicked." Again are they reminded of the gracious offer of freedom from their guilt; freedom from the wrath; freedom from the liability to be treated as enemies; freedom from sin, Satan, and the grave; all comprised in the person of Jesus, receiving whom they receive the whole. James encourages them to come unto him whom they have to speak of with reverence; to call upon his name who never yet refused a suppliant. Then will they be judged, not by rigid, unsparing justice, but by the gentle, loving hand of mercy!

"What the profit, my brethren, if one say he has faith, but have not works? can this faith save him?"

Probably every one on reading this verse considers that Christian faith is here mentioned; that is, faith in our Lord Jesus Christ. If this were the true interpretation, what becomes of the promise, "Believe on

D

the Lord Jesus Christ, and thou shalt be saved"? "Ye are all children of God by faith in Christ Jesus"? (Gal. iii. 36). Scripture cannot contradict Scripture. Any apparent contrariety disappears before a careful examination.*

Throughout the Old Testament Scriptures do we not find a constant demand on the part of God that his people should trust in him? Adam, Abel, Noah, Abraham, Moses, etc., etc., were all believers in God. They trusted him, had faith in him. Hebrews xi. contains an account of many others who had faith in God, apart from Christian faith. Paul, adverting to the faith of Israel, says, in Acts xxvi. 7, "Unto which [promise] our twelve tribes, instantly serving [God] day and night, hope to come." Faith in Christ, or the Christ, though very fully contained in the Old Testament, and most probably possessed by many in that dispensation, was not, however, the declared footing on which the nation was called out of Egypt, brought to mount Sinai, and, through Joshua, put in possession of the promised land. It was faith in God, the God of Israel. It is nevertheless true that their future and permanent possession of that land does depend upon their faith in Christ Jesus, the Son of God.

* In our English version the omission of the definite article, *the* or *this* faith, throws the whole verse into confusion. It is not a question about faith in the abstract, but about faith of this particular kind, whether it can save. The same may be noticed in Luke xviii. 8, where our Lord, after giving out the parable of the unjust judge, is made to say, "Nevertheless when the Son of man cometh, shall he find faith on the earth?" Whereas what he really does say is, "But when the Son of man cometh shall he find the or this faith on the earth?" meaning such faith as that of the poor widow depicted in the narrative.

But in this particular passage I apprehend it is not the intention of the apostle to distinguish between the faith of the Jew and that of the Christian; but to establish that, if faith in God be avowed by an Israelite, it must, in order to be genuine, be accompanied by conduct evincing that faith. Bearing in mind the excessive importance then attached to works, "The man that doeth them shall live in them," or by them, the absence of such works would indicate that there was towards God no stimulus of life in the soul. And that, whatever the protestation might be, the reality of faith was absent. Their God had often spoken to this effect, "They that trust in the Lord shall be as mount Sion, which cannot be moved" (Ps. cxxv. 1); "He shall save them because they trust in him" (Ps. xxxvii. 40).

"But if a brother or a sister be naked, and be destitute of daily food, and one of you say to them, Go in peace, be warmed and filled, but give them not the things needful for the body, what is the profit? So the faith, if it have not works, is dead in itself."

This illustration shows that an expression of compassion and goodwill towards the necessitous, if unattended with an effort to relieve, is of no profit to the needy one; and, consequently, he who might have been the giver obtains not the blessing from God, as promised in Deuteronomy xv. 10, "Thou shalt surely give him, and thine heart shalt not be grieved when thou givest unto him: because that for this thing the Lord thy God shall bless thee in all thy works, and in all that thou puttest thine hand unto."

In the same way, such faith as is described above, whatever may be the protestation of confidence in God, unless accompanied by acts of faith, yields no glory to God, and brings no blessing on the soul. It is dead, not living faith—inoperative—a pretence without the reality. Living faith in God always leads to the performance of what he enjoins, as may be noticed repeatedly in the narratives of the Old Testament.

"But one will say, Thou hast faith and I have works. Show me thy faith without works, and I by my works will show thee my faith."

The statement and demand in this verse seem intended in refutation of the supposed declaration in verse 14, where one is represented as saying he has faith while he has not works. An objector, taking up the assertion, asks him to give evidence of his faith since he has no works to adduce. It is of course impossible for him to prove that he has faith. The objector, contrasting this with his own position, adds, "I have works," and by means of what I have done I can show the faith that actuated me in the performance of those works. It is put here as a question between man and man in order to establish the absurdity of such an antinomian assumption. If man's understanding can perceive this, how much more clearly must he who searches the heart discern it!

Perhaps among the audience who were listening to our Lord's discourse in Matthew xxiii., where he exposes the various sins of scribe and Pharisee, we may imagine that one of them, thus unmasked, and unable to rebut the evidence of guilt, might say to himself, "Though I have nothing to bring forward in the way of conduct whereby to justify myself in the sight of God or man, yet I do maintain that I have faith in the God of Israel. Though I do devour widow's houses, and for a pretence make long prayers, yet do I not sit in Moses' seat, and expound his doctrines? Am I not regular in temple worship, and precise in all the formularies? and could I do this without having faith?" The reply is, the conduct indicates the way the heart is actuated; that evil courses proceed from the heart; and that hypocrisy puts on any disguise that may tend to cover up its designs.

"Thou believest that God is one. Thou doest well! The devils also believe [this] and tremble."

An intelligent Israelite could not but see and avow the oneness of God. Since the captivity in Babylon, the Jew had ceased to worship idols, making his boast over idolaters in the monotheism he now held. But his actions were little influenced by this opinion. Neither from what follows in the further part of this epistle, does the conduct of the Twelve Tribes appear to be any better. In this respect the demons or devils resemble them. But these are terrified at the fact of which they are conscious, whereas Israel is not alarmed. Both persist in their own courses, regardless of the oneness of God. The devils tremble, though they do not obey. Israel neither obeys nor trembles. And hereby their faith is shown to be beneath that of the devils.

"But art thou willing to know, O vain man, that the faith without works is dead." Israel is not willing to learn this important fact. An empty show of reverence is far more congenial to the natural heart than the real reverence which God is entitled to expect from his creature. "If I be a father, where is mine honour? if I be a master, where is my fear?" God does not recognise anything as faith which does not produce reverence and obedience. It has in it no vitality; it is dead.

"Was not Abraham, our father, justified by works, having offered Isaac his son upon the altar? Thou seest that faith wrought with his works, and by the works was the faith completed. And the scripture was fulfilled which said, But Abraham believed God, and it was accounted to him for righteousness; and he was called God's friend."

Several things come under our notice in these verses. The title "our father" given to Abraham, clearly shows that it is still to the Twelve Tribes, not to Gentiles, that James is writing. Though God is the God of the Gentiles as well as of the Jews, yet Abraham is not their father. He is figuratively father of all those who believe, inasmuch as he lived at an earlier period; but he was not their progenitor.

Justification by works being the principle and pivot of the Mosaic code, all Israel seeking to establish their own righteousness, the idea here presented to them by a Christian teacher, of any one being justified by works, and especially their great ancestor, must have been very welcome and consolatory to their minds. God had long before said, "Their righteousness is of me." But now to find the fond wish of their heart apparently corroborated by a servant of Christ, must have been peculiarly gratifying. It is true, when he explains himself there is not much ground for boasting, though at first he seems to concede the whole question.

JAMES II. 20-23.

There is a point of some importance to be noticed. The transaction in Abraham's life here mentioned is recorded in Genesis xxii.; whereas in Genesis xv., many years previously, God had already accounted him righteous. The events in Genesis xv. occurred before the birth of Ishmael, who was fourteen years old when Isaac was born. Since at the time of the sacrifice Isaac was able to carry a load of firewood, he could not well have been less than ten years of age; so that Abraham had already been declared righteous about a quarter of a century before the time when James speaks of him. He could not, therefore, owe his justification to this last event.

Moreover, James refers to his faith as working with his works. It is evident that his works did not originate his faith. They followed in consequence of the faith he already possessed. And these works, the offering up of his son Isaac, were a clear, full, and most marvellous exhibition of his faith in the living God.

And, further, it is to be remarked that both these events were long antecedent to the time of Moses, and consequently to the giving of the law. They were not to be classed with law-works, the only kind which Israel knew, since the law did not then exist. The code was not then embodied, nor given forth. Therefore the class of works by which James says he was justified had no relation to those by which Israel sought justification. In Abraham it was the obedience of faith, the faith of one already justified before God on other grounds. And this act was an evidence of the faith that was in him, and which had occasioned his having been declared righteous. So that the concession James now seems to make to the national feeling, does in reality subvert the national hope of attaining a righteousness of their own.

In the list of eminent servants of God given in Hebrews xi., where the faith of each is spoken of, and likewise the instances of conduct arising from that faith, it will be observed that not one of the instances is a fulfilment of the law of Moses, and consequently not a law work. Most of the named cases are acts of obedience to a specific command to the individual, the personal faith of each being recorded. In each the faith was completed by the act, without which it would have been a dead or inoperative faith, producing no results.

"You see then that by works man is justified, and not by faith only."

The same principle is reiterated; a reprobation of the kind of faith treated of from verse 14 to 20, rectifying the idea thereof in the disputant; and taking away from him the vain plea and hope that a faith without works can save him.

"But likewise was not also Rahab the harlot justified by works, having received the messengers, and having sent them forth another way?"

In this case also Rahab, being a Gentile, and of the race of Canaan, had no relation to the law of Moses. Yet was she justified by an operative faith, which led her to receive and preserve the servants of the God of Israel, in opposition to her own nationality, and endangering her own life by protecting the enemies of her king. There was in her no morality which could assist the expectation of being saved from the sword. It was simply faith in God, working certain results, everything being against her.

"For as the body without spirit is dead, so also the faith without the works is dead."

This last verse completes the explanation. There is no question that the body without spirit is dead. This is self-evident and palpable. So also a faith without corresponding works is dead. This kind of faith has no life in it.

It is plainly to be seen that James has been combating against a pretended and spurious faith, which, being outwardly ostentatious and imposing, leaves the man at liberty to do as he pleases. In its grandest form it is to be seen in 2 Chron. xiii., where Judah and Israel being at war, and the armies in battle array against each other, the king of Judah makes a solemn speech to his antagonists. He charges them with idolatry, and violation of God's arrangements as to kingship and priesthood. Then he declares that himself and Judah have not forsaken the Lord their God, but that the Aaronic priests burn sacrifices and incense, morning and evening, offering the shewbread upon the pure table, with lights upon the golden candlestick, as appointed. All this was outwardly true, and has the aspect of being uttered by a conscientious and zealous servant of God. But in reality it was far otherwise; for in 1 Kings xv. 3 it is recorded of this same Abijah or Abijam, that he walked in all the sins of his father; who, with Judah, his people, had thoroughly lapsed into idolatry, as noted in 1 Kings xiv. 22-24. And there he stands with a brazen face, accusing others of idolatry, while his own land is full of idols under every green tree. The one point, that they still carried on the ritual worship of Jehovah, only made their guilt the more glaring, while they used it as a political pretext against their adversaries.

CHAPTER III.

"Let not many become teachers, my brethren, knowing that we shall receive a greater condemnation. For in many things we all stumble."

The word διδάσκαλος, rendered in our version "Master," literally teacher, is in John i. 38 declared to be equivalent to Rabbi; and it seems throughout this chapter to have this force, and prominently to bring forward this well-known class of persons. The Rabbi was not necessarily of the priestly family. Any one who had sufficient learning might become a Rabbi, and was thereby elevated into a position of dignity and importance above his fellows. To be a teacher of others is to fulfil a laudable and useful service; but we know how soon the function is exalted into an office, and while the office confers dignity on him who fills it, the service itself, as well as the capacity to fulfil it, are liable to degradation. The amount of information possessed, with the capacity and diligence to impart, would be a surer criterion of usefulness in a teacher, than any rank or title he may assume, or which may be conferred upon him by others. He who posseses an official sanction to teach is placed in a position dangerous to himself and others.

James seems here to be treating on the same point with Paul in Rom. i. 32 and ii. 1; where it is declared that the intelligence to discern the right path, unless it be followed, only makes condemnation more certain. Here there is an addition,—*greater* condemnation. The principle as enunciated by our Lord in Luke xii. 47, seems not limited to Israel, but to be of general application. "That servant who knew his Lord's will, and prepared not, neither did according to his will, shall be beaten with many [stripes]." The Rabbi stumbles as well as his neighbour. His elevation makes his fall more conspicuous, and also entails upon him greater condemnation.

"If any one stumbles not in word, this is a perfect man, able to bridle also the whole body."

Judging from the instances recorded in Scripture of faithful servants of God grievously afflicted in person, or much harassed by enemies, we discern amongst the eminent qualities they displayed, some failure in this one point,—the government of the tongue. Job, with all the fortitude and submission he showed under his heavy bereavements, yet "cursed his day." Jeremiah, bold, faithful, and enduring as he was, gave vent to his feelings in the same way. David, with the beautiful self-control he exhibited towards Saul, was on one occasion unable to restrain himself from cursing (1 Sam. xxvi. 19). Even Moses, the meekest man in all the earth, spake unadvisedly with his lips. There was, however, One, the holy One of God, "who when he was reviled, reviled not again; when he suffered, he threatened not; but committed himself unto him who judgeth righteously." The psalmist, admonishing on this subject, says, "What man desires life, loveth days that he may see good? Keep thy tongue from evil, and thy lips from speaking guile."

"Behold, we put the bits in the mouths of the horses, that they may obey us; and we turn their whole body. Behold, also, the ships, being so large and driven with strong winds, are turned with a very small helm, whither the director may will. So also the tongue is a little member and boasts greatly."

From what follows, it would appear that the "boasting" in this passage is not to be understood in a bad sense; but that the tongue, though but a little member of the whole body, is capable of doing great things. The controlling a horse, or the guiding a ship in a storm, are things necessary and useful; and where there is a hand to manage the bit, or use the helm, the value of these small things is apparent. So the tongue, under wise governance, is an instrument of immense importance.

"Behold! how much wood a little fire kindles. And the tongue is fire, a world of injustice. The tongue is set in our members, soiling the whole body, and setting on fire the circle of creation, and being set on fire by hell."

All this has come upon us owing to the pride and audacity actuating our poor ruined race, and the hardihood with which we have dared to say, "Our lips are our own! Who is lord over us?" As in Romans i. 26, 28, because we did not like to retain an acknowledgment of God, he gave us over to this misuse of one of his most surprising gifts and endowments. Where it might be perilous openly to attack, the creature of God is found employing this beneficent endowment in vomiting forth evil against his fellows. Out of the heart proceed evil thoughts. Out of the abundance of the heart the mouth speaketh. And Satan having the mastery of the heart, thus uses it to inflame man against man throughout the wide world. One single word, it may be, spoken in malice or in ridicule, falling among the touchwood of the heart, sets on fire nation against nation, family against family, and members of the same family against each other! It matters not whether the word be true or false, the tongue does not pause to consider this; but, once uttered, the mischief is set in motion and rolls on.

"For every nature of wild beasts and birds, creeping things and marine animals is tamed and has been tamed by human nature. But the tongue can no one of men tame; an unruly evil, full of death-bearing poison."

Man, mentally superior to the brute creation, though inferior in bodily strength to many of them, has succeeded in establishing control over the huge elephant, the fierce and mighty lion and tiger. He has tamed the falcon and the eagle. The deadly serpent has also submitted itself to his command; and fishes also have been taught to come at his bidding. But he has not succeeded in taming himself. The little, unruly member will break through all restraint. So long since as the time of David, the Spirit of God gave this account of the favoured house of Israel: "Their throat is an open sepulchre; with their tongues they have used deceit; the poison of asps is under their lips. And Paul, in Romans iii., declares that in his day this description was equally applicable.

The light in which God regards all this is taught us in the book of Proverbs vi. 16, etc.: "These six things doth the Lord hate: yea, seven are an abomination unto him: a proud look, a lying tongue, and hands that shed innocent blood, a heart that deviseth wicked imaginations, feet that be swift in running to mischief, a false witness that speaketh lies, and he that soweth discord among brethren."

In the days that are coming all this will be rectified. For in Psalm ci., Messiah speaking to his Father, says, "A froward heart shall depart from me: I will not know a wicked person. Whoso privily slandereth his neighbour, him will I cut off: him that hath a high look and a proud heart I will not suffer. He that worketh deceit shall not dwell within my house; he that telleth lies shall not tarry in my sight."

"Therewith bless we the God and Father, and therewith curse we men, made after the likeness of God. Out of the same mouth proceedeth blessing and cursing. My brethren, these things ought not so to be."

God had long condescended to call himself the God of Israel. He had likewise frequently declared himself their Father (Exod. iv. 22; Deut. xxxii. 6; Jer. xxxi. 9). They had understood and boasted in the position thus given them; for in addressing our Lord (John viii. 41), the Jews said, "We have one Father, God." They were, however, by no means careful to yield the requisite obedience, for in Malachi i. 6, God makes this appeal, "A son honoureth his father, and a servant his master. If then I be a father, where is mine honour?" Israel also blessed God as their Father, by the mouth of David, in 1 Chronicles xxix. 10. The way they cursed men may be inferred from the psalm cited by Paul, Romans iii. 14, "Whose mouth is full of cursing and bitterness." That men are made after the likeness of God may be seen in Genesis i. 26, 27. It is not for the creature to curse man, and at the same time profess reverence to him who made him. Those whom God has blessed it is not for man to curse. Balaam was constrained to admit this; and God having blessed our first parents (Gen. i. 22), man cannot reverse it. Well may the apostle say, "These things ought not so to be."

"Doth a fountain from the same opening yield sweet water and bitter? Can a fig-tree, my brethren, bear olives, or a vine figs? So can no fountain yield salt water and sweet."

Perhaps there may be here some remote allusion to Jotham's parable in Judges ix., where the vine, the fig-tree, and the olive, are all introduced, indicating the power to exhilarate, to communicate sweetness and well-being. Each tree has, however, its own nature. It does not produce that which is incongruous to its own special office. Sweet or pure water is intended to fertilize; salt water induces barrenness. The human heart, intended to be the channel of blessing, ought not to be turned from its assigned purpose, to become a source of mischief to others. Such never happens in a fountain. It is intended to convey blessing, not cursing. From the fountain of God's heart there perpetually flows forth a pure stream of mercy and goodwill to man.

"Who among you is wise and learned, let him show his works by good conduct, in a wise meekness. But if ye have bitter envy and strife in your heart, boast not nor lie against the truth. This wisdom descendeth not from above, but is earthly, sensual, demoniacal: for where envy and strife [are], there is disturbance and every evil work."

The conspicuous feature of a Rabbi, highmindedness, leads him naturally into collision with other Rabbis. The envy and strife engendered by each claiming superiority in wisdom and learning, thereby hoping to attract partisans, leads to general disturbance and other fruits of the carnal heart. The desire of being called Rabbi was great in our Lord's time on earth, nor has it yet ceased either in Israel, or outside of Israel.

But if any one wishes to acquire this distinction, the Christian teacher instructs him to pursue an opposite course. He is neither to exhibit nor nourish envy or strife, but to display his wisdom and learning in conduct regulated by these principles, accompanied by a meekness of spirit contrasted with the assumption and haughtiness of the others. "A meek and quiet spirit is in the sight of God of great value," says another Christian teacher writing to sojourners dispersed in certain localities.

The allowance of envy and strife, far from indicating a mind subject to God, is in opposition to the grand requirement dwelt upon in the second chapter of this epistle, "Thou shalt love thy neighbour as thyself." To give way thus is to lie against the truth, to falsify the assumed position, and is none other than the indulgence of what the Law was enacted to restrain and suppress. There is nothing of heaven in such a course; it is simply man's desire, set on fire from below.

"But the wisdom from above, first indeed is pure, then peaceable, gentle, easy to be persuaded, full of mercy and good fruits, impartial, undisguised."

That the purity here mentioned is not pureness of knowledge or intelligence in divine truth is evident, for no such idea has occurred in the epistle. And further, it is plain that the knowledge in those addressed, even of their own scriptures, was but scanty, merely rudimentary, could even so much be advanced in their behalf. Besides, the question is not about knowledge, but wisdom, heavenly wisdom, contrasted with that which is earthly or Satanic.

The purity here contemplated is clearly not that of the intellect, but of a heart devoid of those evil passions just named, the envy and strife, which when raging therein operate through the tongue, defiling the whole body. The mere absence of these things would occasion vacuity, unless other qualities were present. Peaceableness is one grand characteristic. Wisdom's "ways are ways of pleasantness, and all her paths are peace."

Then follow gentleness, and easiness to be persuaded, in contrast with obduracy; full of mercy and good fruits, instead of bitterness and strife; impartiality, as opposed to the conduct condemned in Chapter ii., a preference of the rich to the poor brother; and finally, pellucidness of character, not deceitful nor fraudulent. All these emanate from, and are indications of, wisdom from above. They are amplifications of the Second Table from mount Sinai, regulating intercourse between man and man. They do not rise to the level of the First Table, nor even approach the high topic of the love of God; but it would be well, nevertheless, if attention were given to these admonitions, though the fruits of the Spirit, as given in Galatians v., soar far above them.

"But the fruit of righteousness is sown in peace by the peacemakers."

In the three points here mentioned the effect is traced back to the cause. Fruit of righteousness, or righteous fruit, is what the God of Israel desired of his people, and came to seek among them (Isa. v. 7). He was disappointed. He sought for brotherly love among them, but found neither judgment nor righteousness. The strong were oppressing the weak, who were crying out under their sufferings. Plausible pretences were afterwards made, only however in external display; the vile hypocrisy being detected and exposed by our Lord in Matthew xxiii.

Yet here James is giving some indications of the right course of procedure, if, it may be, they will so far avail themselves of it. That which is pleasing to God cannot be wrought by a contentious, angry spirit. "The wrath of man worketh not the righteousness of God." Only the peacemaker can produce it. And even he must do it in a peaceful way, or his work is vitiated. The owner of a field, on beholding a fine crop of wheat, evenly grown and well matured, discerns at once that the labourer he employed was not a man of fiery passions, but a man of peace; and that while he scattered the seed his mind was not agitated nor excited, but tranquil. Otherwise there would have been an irregular distribution of the grain, and a consequent irregularity in the growth. So, as a preliminary,—an indispensable preliminary to the production of any fruit unto God, the soul must be imbued with the desire for peace, and must also seek to accomplish the object in a peaceable way. The exhortations thus far given would be merely a clearing away of some of the thorn-bushes and stumbling-blocks lying in the path, sufficient to furnish guidance for the footsteps, if there were a desire to proceed. But the servant of God and of Christ could not then venture to state what he knew and desired to tell of him, the True Vine, apart from whom no fruit could be brought forth such as could be acceptable to God.

CHAPTER IV.

"Whence [are] wars and whence battles among you? [Are they] not hence, of your lusts that wage war in your members? Ye long for, and have not: ye murder and envy, and are not able to obtain: ye fight and war, but ye have not, because ye ask not. Ye ask and receive not, because ye ask wickedly, that ye may spend upon your lusts."

Having expostulated thus strongly against the abuse of the tongue, James now turns to a still darker feature. The state of society as disclosed in this passage is most alarming. Given up to riotous pleasures, full of envy, grasping at that which belongs not to them, and even murdering the owner for the plunder. Tumultuous, rushing to arms, fighting battles, not as being summoned by the authorities, but from unrestrained licence of disposition. Some of these things are identical with what God charges upon them in Isaiah i.: "Thy princes are rebellious, companions of thieves." "Your hands are full of blood." "How is the faithful city become a harlot! it was full of judgment; righteousness lodged in it; but now murderers." Zephaniah iii. 3, also tells the same dismal tale: "Her princes within her are roaring lions; her judges are evening wolves; they gnaw not the bones till the morrow. Her prophets are light and treacherous persons; her priests have polluted the sanctuary, they have done violence to the law." A more lawless state of things could not well exist than is here depicted in the royal city of David, the chosen city where the God of Israel had been pleased to place his name. So demoralized indeed was Israel, even under her best kings, that Solomon deems it necessary to caution his son, perhaps his heir-apparent, in this way: "My son, if sinners entice thee, consent thou not. If they say, 'Come with us, let us lay wait for blood, let us lurk privily for the innocent without cause: let us swallow them up alive as the grave; and whole as those that go down into the pit: we shall find all precious substance, we shall fill our houses with spoil: cast in thy lot among us; let us all have one purse:' My son, walk not thou in the way with them; refrain thy foot from their path."

Were we to seek among the worst governed countries

of Europe for a parallel with this in princes and people, we should not find it; scarcely even in Asia, save among the Afghans, the descendants of this very race. Some of the savage tribes of Central Africa might perhaps furnish the parallel case. Thus low had Israel sunk. From the strength of James's language, it would appear that the people carried away with them into their dispersion these national characteristics; which may also throw light upon the proneness of the Jews to tumultuous deeds of violence and secret treachery in the time of our Lord.

The history of the Jews in Syria, Asia Minor, and Egypt, subsequent to the destruction of Jerusalem by Titus, accords with the apostle's description. Ever rising up in tumult against their fellow-citizens, slaying thousands and tens of thousands of them. The violence brought upon themselves, eventually, most terrible retribution.

In regard to the possibility of persons of this description asking of God, and not receiving, we have these declarations from his word: "He that turneth away his ear from hearing the Law, even his prayer shall be abomination." "The sacrifice of the wicked is an abomination to the Lord."

"Ye adulteresses,* know ye not that the friendship of the world is enmity with God? whoever therefore wills to be a friend of the world is an enemy of God."

The truth here taught is very similar to that in 1 John ii. 15, with this difference, that John speaks of the less glaring aspect of the world and its ways

* So all the old MSS.

as opposed to God; whilst here James is dwelling upon its open violence and profligacy; those to whom he writes being at a much lower stage of degradation. But the sinner, whether refined or sensual, peaceable or violent, is still an enemy of God; and will reap the results of his enmity. "The course of this world" (Eph. ii. 2) may vary according to the temper of the age, the progress of civilization and refinement at different epochs or in different countries; but the course of this world is still a state of ruin, opposition to God and his Christ, and of subjection to Satan. He that cultivates its friendship turns his back upon God! This is the adultery here charged upon Israel, whom God claims (Isa. liv. 5), as having been united to himself, and whom he often by his prophets charges with adultery against him.

"Or think ye that the Scripture says in vain, The spirit that dwells in us yearns toward envy? But greater is the favour he gives. Wherefore he saith, God resists the proud, but to the humble he gives favour. Submit therefore to God. Resist the devil, and he will flee from you."

Have you not been forewarned of old respecting the evil heart of man, that its tendencies are not towards, but against his fellow-man? Ambitious to exalt itself above him, covetous in grasping at that which belongs to him, and ready to slay if he will not submit himself or yield up his goods! These and other evil passions raging in the breast, lead to all the wickedness and violence that has been named. But God is able to enable you to conquer these passions. Submit therefore to him. Until this be done, he cannot regard you as humble; and you cannot therefore expect from him the favour requisite to make you victorious. Resist the devil, who has hitherto found you pliant and at his disposal, and he will flee from you. But why should he flee? Because he sees God near at hand to help all who submit themselves to him. Remember his promise in Deuteronomy iv. 29: "But if from thence (the dispersion among the Gentiles) thou shalt seek the Lord thy God, thou shalt find him, if thou seek him with all thy heart and with thy soul. When thou art in tribulation, and all these things are come upon thee in the latter days, if thou turn to the Lord thy God, and be obedient to his voice, (for the Lord thy God is a merciful God,) he will not forsake thee, neither destroy thee, nor forget the covenant of thy fathers which he sware unto them."

"Draw nigh to God, and he will draw nigh to you. Cleanse [your] hands, [ye] sinners; purify your hearts, [ye] double-minded. Be afflicted, and mourn, and weep: let your laughter be turned to mourning, and the joy to heaviness. Humble yourselves before God, and he will raise you up."

In 2 Chronicles xv. 2, God was pleased to repeat the promise to Judah and Benjamin,—"The Lord is with you while ye be with him; and if ye seek him, he will be found of you; but if ye forsake him, he will forsake you." Another gracious promise is contained in Joel ii. 14-19, coupled with an exhortation somewhat similar to the present. God waits to be gracious to the house of Israel on their thus humbling themselves before him,—an acting of mercy beyond all measure deep and overflowing.

The promise here made is a renewal of what the God of Israel had so often been pleased to repeat to his people, and which he had so repeatedly fulfilled when they humbled themselves before him. Among the many passages to this effect may be noticed especially Lev. xxvi. 41 ; 2 Kings xxii. 19; 2 Chron. xii. 6, and xxxiv. 27; Isa. lvii. 15; together with the wonderful cases of Ahab, Manasseh, and Nebuchadnezzar the Gentile. Far greater still is the blessing to him who now humbles himself before Jesus, the crucified and risen Son of God.

"Speak not against one another, brethren. He who speaks against his brother, and judges his brother, speaks against the Law, and judges the Law. But if thou judgest the law, thou art not a law-doer, but a judge. The Lawgiver and Judge is one who is able to save and to destroy! Who art thou that judgest the other?"

Again James recurs to the misuse of the tongue; and this time with striking reference to Israel's peculiar position. God had commanded each to love his neighbour as himself. And one, therefore, who speaks against his brother, and judges him (to be a wrongdoer), not only breaks the law, but virtually declares himself right in so doing. That is to say, he by his act condemns the law which forbids him so to do; thereby abandoning his position as a servant under the law, and usurping another position which belongs not to him, that of condemning the law as unsuitable. The Lawgiver, however, is not Moses, but God, who is also the Judge of all. He discerns who has violated his commands, and who has obeyed them. He is able to save, if he sees fit, those whom man condemns. And he is able to destroy any accuser who thus exalts himself in violation of his commands. Who art thou who judgest the other? forgetting that "thou doest the same things."

The language of Psalm xiv. seems still present in the apostle's mind: "Whose mouth is full of cursing and bitterness." The prevalence of this habit in Israel is very noticeable. These among other instances are recorded. Joshua (Josh. vi. 26); Israel (Jud. xxi. 18); Saul (1 Sam. xiv. 24); David (1 Sam. xxvi. 19); Elisha (2 Kings ii. 24); Nehemiah (Neh. xiii. 25); Jeremiah (Jer. xx. 14); the Pharisees (John vii. 49). From Psalm cix. 17, 18, it seems to have been an universal tendency in Israel.

"Come now ye who say, To-day and to-morrow we will go unto such a city, and stay there one year, and trade and get gain: whereas ye know not what [will be] on the morrow. For what is your life? For it is a vapour, which appears for a little time, but then disappears. Instead of your saying, If the Lord will, and we should live, and do this or that. But now ye exult in your boastings: all such exulting is evil."

It had been long ago said by Solomon, "Boast not thyself of to-morrow, for thou knowest not what a day may bring forth." But the sons of men heed not the admonition. One and all grasp the morrow as a certainty, laying their plans accordingly. And yet our existence is as dependent as it ever was upon the pleasure of him who created and maintains it. All treating the morrow as if it were already our own, is bad, since it ignores him by whom we live, move, and exist.

Like a little mist in the air, which presently is dissolved, such is human life. None can keep alive his own soul, nor redeem his brother from the grave.

"Therefore, to him who knows to do good, and does it not, to him it is sin."

The knowledge of what is right, if unattended by the practice, does in no wise exculpate. It only adds sin to sin; as is clearly declared in Mark xii. 47. And yet no refuge is to be found in ignorance, as the next verse shows. He who was under the Law must obey every jot and tittle of it, or incur sin and the divine displeasure. The Gentiles who have not the Law, have the light of conscience, and by its dictates, undisturbed by human traditions, they are to govern themselves. Whereas the Christian, subject to Christ, has to regulate himself according to all that his Master has been pleased to command.

We have just seen how penetrating and how searching is the word when explained in its true bearing. In our Lord's sermon on the Mount many enactments of the Law are so explained; showing that whilst the outward points embraced were specific and distinctly marked, yet the interior designs reached far deeper. Although a conscientious, moral, and earnest mind might say with truth, "All these things have I kept from my youth up," so far as the common acceptation of their requirements extended; yet when the practical test respecting love to the neighbour was presented, in the naked form of making a distribution of his property among them, the fallacy is at once detected; and the unhappy fact is disclosed, that he has not loved, and does not love, his neighbour as himself.

In like manner in this epistle the deeper significancy of this law has been shown both in chapter ii. 1–9 by another simple test, that of giving the neighbour an inferior seat or none.

And again, by the speaking against a brother, it is made apparent that the speaker does not love him as he loves himself. So that by all these instances it is made self-evident that the man has not done what he knows he ought to have done, and that thereby he has committed sin. The immediate conclusion cannot be avoided, that he has broken the Law, and is therefore under the curse announced in Deuteronomy xxvii. 26, as cited by Paul in Galatians iii. 10: "Cursed is every one who continueth not in all things which are written in the book of the law to do them." This fearful position, so crushing to the heart and hopes of the Israelite, is not here stated in words. It is the inevitable conclusion to which the argument shuts them up; a discovery to be made and applied to himself by each one.

Apparently the design is to make palpable, and press home the bitter fact that, if they desire to be saved from the curse and the coming wrath, they must look for safety elsewhere than to law-keeping; for through this channel there is no hope of obtaining righteousness. Having brought them to this point, he leaves the rest to conscience. He cannot venture to be more explicit.

CHAPTER V.

"Come now the rich! Weep; howling over your miseries which are coming. Your wealth has decayed, and your garments have become moth-eaten. Your gold and silver is rusted, and the rust of them will be for testimony to you, and will eat your flesh as fire. Ye have stored up for the last days. Behold the hire of the labourers who have reaped your fields, withheld by you, crieth; and the cries of the reapers have entered into the ears of the Lord of sabaôth. Ye have luxuriated upon the earth, and run riot. Ye have nourished your hearts as in a day of slaying. Ye have condemned, murdered the Just One: he does not oppose you."

The subject now turns to the calamities coming upon the rich. The tendency to honour wealth, however acquired, has been already noticed in the second chapter; and likewise the tendency in the wealthy to oppress those under their control. So common is the characteristic, that in the Old Testament the terms seem almost synonymous; to be rich is to be an oppressor.

Among savage nations, strength of arms and daring lead to eminence and the acquisition of property. In those which are semi-civilized, as Israel, the possessor of wealth can offer protection and sustenance to the poor, who thereby become his dependants, and enable him to gratify both ambition and avarice, to the detriment of others. Under any circumstances, the tendency never seems to depart from the heart of man. In settled communities the laws restrain its exercise; but it can only be subdued in those who are imitators of him "who, though he was rich, yet for our sakes became poor, that we through his poverty might be made rich."

Whereas the desire of God's heart was to find his people Israel abounding in love towards one another, he has left it on record that all were oppressors! Kings, princes, and people, all doers of wrong to each other, according to their opportunities. Isaiah i. and v. and Ezekiel xxxiv. fully show this hateful feature. In Habakkuk ii., the Lord is pleased to announce the fearful results. " Woe to him who increaseth that which is not his." " Woe to him who coveteth an evil covetousness to his house, that he may set his nest on high, and be delivered from the power of evil." " Woe to him who buildeth a town with blood, and establisheth a city by iniquity."

To these woes James now adverts. He warns them that not only will the wealth disappear, but that that which remains will be a testimony to them of the unerring judgment of God, under the agony of which the sting of conscious guilt will eat into their flesh as fire. Jeremiah xvii. 11, testifies to the same point. Isaiah xlix. 9, and li. 8, speaks of the moth-eaten garment. So long back as Deuteronomy xxiv. 14, 15, God had declared to them that if the labourer was not paid his wages, and in consequence cried to the Lord, his master would incur sin. Disregarding all these solemn admonitions, we perceive that in James's day they were practising the very same thing, and that the cries of the oppressed had entered into the ears of the Lord of hosts, a title by which God had often announced himself to Israel. So reckless were they of consequences, that the language of Isaiah xxii. 12, 13, closely describes their then condition of soul : " And in that day did the Lord God of hosts call to weeping, and to mourning, and to baldness, and to girding with sackcloth; and behold, joy and gladness, slaying oxen, and killing sheep, eating flesh, and drinking wine: let us eat and drink, for to-morrow we die."

In addition to all their other crimes, the nation was now involved in the traitorous murder of their king, and in the denunciations before proclaimed on this account. Herein also was committed a most solemn infraction of the Law (Exod. xxiii. 7). Jesus is not now acting in opposition to them; on the contrary, his heart is still towards them, and his hand still stretched out in mercy. But the time will come "when he shall cry, yea roar; he shall prevail against his enemies."

"Be long-enduring therefore, brethren, until the coming of the Lord! Behold, the husbandman waiteth for the precious fruit of the earth, long-enduring in regard to it, until he receive the early and the latter rain. Be ye also long-enduring, establish your hearts, for the coming of the Lord has approached."

The glorious hope presented to the Church of Christ is that her Lord, who has borne her sins, expiated her guilt in his own life's blood, and gone into the heavens in her behalf, will again come from thence to receive her unto himself and convey her into the presence of his Father, to dwell with him there for ever. This hope belongs to all who trust in him, though few comparatively have known, or laid it to heart. He has said to all who believe on him,—to helpless, worthless sinners like ourselves,—"Because I live, ye shall live also." And he has likewise said, "I go to prepare a place for you." And further, he has expressed to his Father his desire that those whom his Father has given him may be with him where he is. Every one who comes to him he recognises as having been given to him by his Father, and he therefore welcomes them. He will never send away or lose sight of any one of them; for is not each a gift to him by his Father, whom he so tenderly loves, and who has bestowed them on him that they may be cared for throughout eternity?

In the meantime his people are left in a state of suffering and trial here below, and of confession of him as their confidence and hope. He has not yet openly interfered, as he did in respect to Israel in Egypt. They had to wait four hundred years before the day of their rescue came. But it did come. From that day their position was changed. The Church has had to wait much longer; but the day when our Lord comes forth from the heavens, as announced in 1 Thessalonians iv., will terminate her sorrow, and be the commencement of her glory and her joy. From that happy moment she is ever with her Lord. He takes to himself the Bride whom he so dearly loves, whom he has purchased to himself at so costly a price.

Closely allied to this hope, and yet distinct from it, is another,—the hope of Israel. The same Lord has undertaken to do wondrous things for them also. He was born to be their King; and though they disallowed his title, their refusal has neither set it aside nor invalidated it. His claim far from being destroyed, has been greatly enlarged; for Jesus is become

King of kings and Lord of lords: the blessed, the only Potentate. The extent of his dominion comprises heaven as well as earth.

Yet there is one favoured spot on this earth, the scene of his birth, his youth, and his manhood. The only place he visited while here,—a land where he lived for many years in obscurity; which witnessed his arduous labours, his sorrows, his endurance under suffering, his faithfulness to his God and Father, and his martyrdom. It was on the inhabitants of that land his full heart's love was bestowed; and oh! such a heart, and such love as never was known elsewhere. These were the special people of his Father. There was his Father's earthly house; and when all had gone wrong with it and them, he was the One commissioned by his Father to take the reins of government and bring about restoration. When they refused his loving service, there was no anger, no withdrawal on his part. Weeping over the city, he suffered the inhabitants, whom he could have annihilated in a moment, to nail him to a cross and pour out upon his guiltless head the utmost of their fierce, insulting, and ignorant malignity. Even after this, so dear were they still to him, that having risen from the dead, he does not go elsewhere, but appears again on the same place, lingers there for many days, before he retires to that abode of bliss, where alone his person and his service meet with the acceptance they deserve, and where his full heart finds the sympathy it desires.

When he again visits this earth, it is on the same identical spot he first sets his foot. It is thither the ardour of his love brings him to the aid and rescue of the very people who have hitherto with such persistent audacity renounced his authority and despised his person. He has still to fulfil his Father's commission, to raise up the tribes of Jacob and restore the outcasts of Israel. And this he is forward to do.

His coming for this purpose has long been predicted in many passages in the Psalms and the Prophets: so many, indeed, that it is difficult to make a selection, especially as it is not intended here to discuss the subject, but merely to point out that the event was proclaimed by God to the expectation of his people Israel. Zechariah xiv. 4, and Malachi iii. 2, will establish the literality of his personal presence; these, with Isaiah lxii. 11, and Psalm lxviii. 18, the purposes of favour to Israel with which he comes. Isaiah xiii. 9, xl. 10, lxvi. 15, and Habakkuk iii., display the terrors of his majestic appearance, and the outpouring of his wrath against the enemies of Israel. Isaiah xlii. 13, contrasts his future demeanour with the way (Isa. xlii. 2, 3) he acted while formerly on earth. Psalm xcvi. 13, and lxviii. 18, display further purposes of his grace after he has subdued his enemies; and Psalm cxviii. 26, with Isaiah xxv. 9, and Zechariah xii. 10, the welcome Israel will give him on his Second coming.

It is here to be carefully noticed that in all these passages the testimony is that the Lord will come. It is not said who he is. His official capacity is declared, but his personal name is withheld. Not until the incarnation was the personal name of Jesus announced. Israel was very familiar with these prophecies, understood their bearing, expected and desired their fulfilment. They still expect this, and most properly they do so; for hath not God spoken? They stumbled, however, at the tried stone which God had laid in Zion. They would not receive Jesus as Lord. And though Peter, in Acts ii., by the power of the Holy Ghost proves that God had made the same Jesus, whom they had crucified, both Lord and Christ, the nation steadily refused, and to this day does refuse, to acknowledge him as such.

We, who through the mercy of our God, have had our eyes opened and our hearts subdued, do thankfully recognise and own Jesus as our Lord, and the Christ of God. We have consequently been welcomed by him; we have been delivered from the wrath, and saved. But Israel, nationally, like Thomas of old, demands ocular and tangible proof that he is indeed the Christ. This evidence will be furnished to them hereafter, when he comes surrounded with his own glory, the glory of his Father, and that of the holy angels. Then they will submit, and own him. But, through this obduracy, the season for their obtaining the higher, the heavenly inheritance, has passed away, and they must be contented with the earthly blessing through infinite mercy kept in store for them.

James now points to this happy epoch. He does not tell them to wait for the coming of Jesus, but of the Lord; he well knowing and rejoicing in the identity, though they did not. Perhaps, from his using the same tense * of the verb as is employed in Matthew iii. 2, and iv. 17, he may be alluding to the

* ἤγγικε.

proclamation then made, that the kingdom of the heavens had approached; but the main point of his exhortation is to look to the fulfilment yet future.

The early and the latter rain, in expectation of which the Palestine husbandman waits, if anything more is intended here beyond the simple fact, may perhaps point on to what is prophesied in Joel ii. 23. There rain is promised in abundance for the production of wheat, wine, and oil. And also, in verse 28, is the promise of the pouring out of God's Spirit, as referred to by Peter on the day of Pentecost. It may be that the allusion to what then took place is symbolised by the former rain; while the latter and more abundant rain relates to the future pouring forth of the Spirit upon the whole family of Israel; the former embracing only a few of them. The whole passage seems intended to convey comfort to the poor ones suffering under the oppressors, whose conduct has just been denounced and their ruin foretold.

"Groan not against one another, brethren, that ye be not judged. Behold the judge * stood before the doors."

Under the feeling of oppression and injury, what is more natural than to complain, and to groan against the oppressor? We have seen, in Deuteronomy xv. 9, and xxiv. 15, how the ear of the Lord was open when the cry of the poor Israelite went forth against his rich brother. He was ever ready to attend to their groan of distress. But if the poor one felt aggrieved, and thus made his complaint, perhaps his rich neighbour had

---

* πρὸ τῶν θυρῶν ἕστηκεν.

something to allege against him,—some wrong-doing, some theft, some false-dealing, on account of which he too has occasion to groan. The impartial Judge hears both complaints; and, if he finds both are to be blamed, passes his award accordingly. Few are able to go before him with hands entirely clean. Better then not to groan, but to endure as previously exhorted. Another motive to this is added in verse 11.

The verb in the last clause of the sentence being in the past tense, and the noun in the plural number, evidently conveys some further idea than if it were, as in the ordinary version, "standeth before the door." The purport is probably nearly similar, but the words seem to relate to some previous incident familiar to those addressed, and which James thus recalls to their remembrance with the warning it contains. Among the various circumstances in their marvellous history, perhaps the allusion may be to the scene recorded in Numbers xvi., where Korah and others, having gathered all the congregation against Moses and Aaron, on the charge of exalting themselves to the detriment of the rest of Israel, the Lord issued his orders through Moses, that the people should depart from the tents of Dathan and Abiram. These men came out and stood at the door (in the Greek, doors) of their tents, with their wives and little ones. "The earth opened her mouth and swallowed them up and their houses," etc. If this be indeed the incident referred to, it presents a sufficient corroboration of the apostle's admonition.

"Take an example, my brethren, of the suffering affliction and long endurance of the prophets, who spake to you in the name of the Lord."

From the statements in Nehemiah ix. 30, Jeremiah ii. 30, and Acts vii. 52, it is too plain that all the prophets whom God sent to Israel were persecuted by them, and many of them put to death. Two instances may indicate the nature and extent of their affliction and their endurance. In 1 Kings xx., a prophet commands his neighbour by the word of the Lord to smite him, and, in consequence, receives a wound. Wounded as he is, he then proceeds to encounter his king, at the head of his army, all flushed with their recent victory, and to announce to him the heavy judgments God was about to bring upon him. To all appearance the prophet's life hung by a single thread.

Another instance is that of Jeremiah, who for more than forty years continued to discharge the prophetic office, always in opposition to the people and their idolatry, and the greater part of the time in bold conflict with king and princes also; his life ever exposed to their violence. The prophetic office involved renunciation of all the ease and comfort which other men are permitted to enjoy. For them, however, their God has provided a special reward! They were indeed eminent examples of patient endurance, suffering wrongfully; speaking as they did in the name of the Lord.

"Behold, we count those happy who endure. Ye have heard of the endurance of Job, and have seen the end of the Lord, that the Lord is very pitiful and of tender mercy."

The idea conveyed by the word "patience" seems scarcely adequate to what is here intended, meaning only fortitude, resignation, submission. But what is here contemplated is the endurance of danger, privation, and grief, for the sake of God and his service, in obedience to his commands. And man has reason to esteem such persons happy, seeing that their God intends to make them so. The end of the Lord was distinctly seen in the case of Job; for after his time of trial had been passed through, God gave him twice as much as he had before. But in other cases it cannot now be seen. Resurrection has to take place first, and then the reward will follow. Fully will the heart be compensated for all its sufferings here; its sorrow will be turned into joy; and that joy is eternal!

"But before all, my brethren, swear not; neither by heaven, nor by earth, nor by any other oath. But let your yea (be) yea; and your nay, nay; that ye fall not under judgment."

In this passage James seems to have in his mind the injunctions of our blessed Lord contained in Matthew v. 33–37, and xxiii. 16–22. From v. 33, "Thou shalt not forswear thyself, but shalt perform unto the Lord thine oaths." As taken from Numbers xxx. 2, it seems clear that originally the idea was that of a vow. What so natural to a man, if he wishes some favour from Heaven, to promise something in return. From Jacob's vow (Gen. xxviii.) to the present day it has been common to all ages and countries, and is so still. Who of us has not made vows? All such vows are based upon the persuasion that we have the power to fulfil them, and that it is the proper and only course to promise some trifling return in the way of payment for the benefit we desire. If God were pleased in days of old to sanction such things, and also to grant the thing desired, it does not establish the propriety of a vow, but only the amazing condescension of the Most High in deigning to listen to such an offer. Let any subject present such a proposal to his earthly monarch, and see the way it will be viewed. And can it be right in the creature of the dust to offer to buy what he wants from the Creator and Possessor of heaven and of earth? What can he pay that does not already belong to God?

But it would appear that the primary thought and intent had by degrees degenerated into mere forms of expression, such as are often employed at present by persons who fear not God, yet use his name in conversation. Our Lord, in the passage in Matthew, seems to be drawing attention to the import of the language they use, and showing its impropriety; seeking to raise their thoughts out of the common current by showing how the expressions are viewed above; so that, whether a vow is really contemplated or otherwise, its exceeding impropriety may be apparent.

James also appears to be dwelling on the same points, but perhaps with more particular inclination to the vow. For, after he has spoken as above of the distress of the people and their need of endurance, he seems to say, "Now do not attempt to deliver yourselves out of it, as your forefathers did, by making a vow. If you do, you will, from inability to discharge the debt, fall under judgment. Or if you, in light conversation, use these asseverations, you will equally fall under judgment, from the dishonour thereby done to God." He is not here taking up the case of a fraudulent heart, as in Malachi i. 14, which substitutes an inferior offering for that which had been vowed; but that of the careless mind, or of the sincere person who is in earnest. In the next verses the subject becomes a little more clear.

"Is any one among you suffering trouble? let him pray. Is any one glad? let him sing praises."

Following as this injunction does upon the last, it seems to say, Another and a better course remains. Pray. The ear of your God is open to listen. His heart feels for you. He has already said he will never leave nor forsake you; therefore lay your distress before him. Then, if he should be pleased to grant deliverance, and you in consequence are happy in being relieved, your part will be to sing his praises. There will then be no burden upon you about payment of a vow, which would interfere with your gladness, but offer praise to Him to whom the thanksgiving is due.

"Is any among you sick? Let him call for the elders of the assembly, and let them pray over him, anointing him with oil in the name of the Lord; and the prayer of faith will save the invalid, and the Lord will raise him up; and, if he have committed sins, they will be forgiven him."

A third condition, that of sickness, is now taken up; containing instructions and promises in their own nature full of extreme difficulty, inasmuch as they seem neither to accord with the character of the old dispensation, nor with that of the new. True it is the apostles and the seventy disciples were sent out with commission to heal; also in Mark xvi. 18, the gift of healing is promised, and in 1 Corinthians xii. 9, it is stated as already possessed by those gathered to the name of the Lord Jesus. But beyond the period of the outset of the gospel dispensation we do not hear anything more of miraculous healings.

Nothing in the Acts, nor in the Epistles of Paul, seems at all analagous to the instructions here given. Neither the lame man at the temple-gate (Acts ii.), nor the cripple (xiv. 8), had their strength restored by the process here described; nor was Dorcas (ix. 40), nor Eutychus (xx. 9), raised from the dead in this way. Later on, when Paul mentions the sickness and recovery of Epaphroditus (Phil. ii. 27), no mention is made of miraculous healing, nor of anointing with oil, nor of the prayers of persons assembled as James directs. Again, in 2 Timothy iv. 20, Paul says, "Trophimus have I left at Miletum sick." Had either procedure been then available for his restoration, we may fairly conclude that Paul would not have left him in that condition. Timothy is not directed to seek the removal of his "often infirmities" in this way, but by the use of "a little wine."

James speaks as if this were an infallible remedy for disease. But not only have millions upon millions died since then, but also the Epistles speak of the death of the body as universal to all the sons of Adam, except in regard to those who may yet be alive when the Lord comes. Were James's directions applicable to us, and intended to be universal, none need die. The servants of the Lord Jesus, however, as their Master did, depart out of this life unto their Father; either by the sudden severance of the thread of life, or by the gradual progress of decay; awaiting the day of resurrection, when this mortal shall put on immortality, and this corruptible shall put on incorruption. What

Jesus has earned for them and bestows is, not an indefinite prolongation of natural life, but what is far grander, more exalted, more blissful,—the eternal life, in spiritual bodies that cannot die; fitted to enjoy the blaze of the glory in the heavens, the presence of him whose face shines above the brightness of the sun itself.

And though our God may and often does raise up his people in answer to the prayers of themselves or their friends, still this is the exception, not the rule; arising from his sovereign grace, acting independently of the procedure now under consideration.

Again, in respect of the Old Testament dispensation, we read of nothing corresponding with this. Abraham prayed for Abimelech (Gen. xx.); Moses for Miriam (Num. xii.); Hezekiah for his people (2 Chron. xxx. 20); for himself (2 Kings xx.) In all these instances the Lord heard, and restored health; yet we read nothing of elders being summoned, nor of oil being applied.

Their God had promised (Exod. xxiii. 25, and Deut. vii. 11-15), that if Israel served him, and obeyed his orders, he would take away from them all sickness. This gracious pledge was national and persistent: but the ground was altogether distinct from the present subject.

When the Lord Jesus appeared on earth, as the King coming to his subjects, he healed the diseases of all who came to him, exhibiting thereby his divine credentials and displaying his good-will. Sometimes it was done by a word, sometimes by the laying on of his blessed hands, and also in other modes. When, in Luke v., the palsied man was brought into his presence, he tells him to rise and walk; explaining to those around that he had the power not only to heal the disease, but to forgive the sins which had brought on the disease; that is to say, that in the exercise of his divine and royal authority he could both remit the punishment and forgive the crime on account of which the punishment was inflicted. Though the word differed, the effect was identical. The King could employ which form of expression he pleased for the release of his subject. Israel, as we have already seen, was visited both nationally and individually with bodily sicknesses as well as hostile invasion, etc., on failure in obedience, as may further be largely noticed in Leviticus xxvi., Deuteronomy xxviii., Isaiah i., Joel ii. and iii., Haggai, and a multitude of other passages. Vast was the power of their new monarch in being able, not only to remit and exempt them from all punishment, but also to deliver them from further liability by pardoning the guilt itself. All this he will fully accomplish in their behalf in the days to come, as well as very much more when he takes away the stony heart and gives them a heart of flesh (Ezek. xxxvi.).

This power the Lord delegated to his twelve disciples on the occasion of their mission, not to Gentiles or Samaritans, but to Jews alone, in Matthew x., also on another and later occasion, in Luke ix., extending it to seventy more, in Luke x. The " binding and loosing," " remitting and retaining," power for which was conferred upon Peter, in Matthew xvi., and then upon the other disciples, in John xx., seems to be of this identical description; carried out by the powers to heal bestowed upon them at Pentecost, and largely used by them afterwards.

One notice occurs of the twelve employing oil (Mark vi. 13). On this point it may be remarked that oil is largely employed in the East as a lubricant for the person. Every one who can afford it anoints the whole body periodically, on account of the salutary effect. It forms also a principal part of medical treatment. In cases of fever, wounds, and other disorders, it is not unusual to place the patient in a bath of oil, where sometimes he is made to recline for days and even weeks together. On account of the refreshment furnished by oil, it was customary to anoint the heads of guests at an entertainment (Luke vii. 46); and in 2 Chronicles xxviii. 15, the captives were anointed as well as clothed and fed previous to being set free. The good Samaritan pours oil into the wounds of the helpless man, and gives him wine to drink (Luke x. 34).

Another point is remarkable. The invalid is not told to pray for healing, but to send for the elders by whose prayer the cure is to be effected; provided they pray in faith, which seems taken for granted. It thus becomes an official act on the part of the elders, from whose petition God will not turn away.

But who are these Elders of the assembly? The word ἐκκλησία, ecclesia, is generally in the New Testament rendered "Church." But this is by no means the primary meaning of the word, which originally had nothing ecclesiastical in it. It is merely an assembly, and is three times thus used in Acts xix. relative to the tumultuous concourse of the Ephesian citizens. In many places* of the Old Testament it is likewise so

---

* Deut. ix. 10; xviii. 16; Jud. xxi. 8; 1 Sam. xvii. 47; 2 Chron. xxx. 23; Neh. v. 7; Ps. cvii. 32; Prov. v. 14.

employed. It then becomes a question whether it is here to be understood in the ecclesiastical sense, or in that of the Old Testament.

Then as to "the Elders." All through the four Gospels, and in many other passages, the word designates the Elders of the Jews; subsequently it is used for the Elders of the Church. The Elders, throughout the Mosaic law, were recognised in each town and village as possessing certain municipal and magisterial functions.

In writing to the Twelve Tribes in the dispersion, in which sense would James be most likely to employ those two words? Would it not probably be in the way in which the terms were understood by them, and not in the sense with which they were not familiar? Being Elders of Israel, accustomed to synagogue usages (chap. ii. 2), they could, if so minded, make petition in behalf of their suffering brother, anointing him with oil in the name of the Lord God of their fathers. We have already seen his promises when, in foreign lands, his people call upon him.

To me it seems that this special announcement through James partakes of the same character of mercy with the incident recorded in 2 Kings xiii. 21, when a dead body being thrown into the grave of Elisha, as it touched his bones it revived, and the man was restored to life. It showed that though they had forgotten their God, he was still near to them. The superhuman strength wherewith he endowed Samson is another instance of the same. The pool of Bethesda, with the cure effected upon the angel troubling the water, is another. All these being intended practically to teach

Israel the willingness of their God to interfere in their behalf if they would but seek him.

It may possibly be that this message through James was designed to stir up their hearts and lead them back to him, by evincing his readiness to grant their prayer in restoring before their eyes the invalid whose case they could not but know, and for whose recovery they had prayed: so to induce them to ask the still greater things already noted in chapter 1.

The promise to forgive sins and heal the malady, whatever it might be, because of the intercessory prayer of others, is an astonishing proof of divine goodness. We are reminded herein of the frequent appeals to our blessed Lord while on earth, by friends and relatives of diseased persons, and in no case did the sufferer fail of obtaining relief.

But it is plain that such relief pertained only to removal of bodily illness, or the sin which occasioned it. For if it concerned the soul's salvation from the wrath to come, then would all necessity for personal faith in the Lord Jesus be dispensed with; and, more than this, Jesus would have died in vain, if prayer alone, without faith in him, could obtain eternal salvation for the sinner.

"Confess to one another the offences, and pray for one another, so that ye may be healed. The fervent prayer of a righteous man prevaileth much."

The transgressions committed against God seem here intimated. They are not to be kept concealed, but acknowledged; so that those who pray may have the facts before their mind, and frame their petitions accordingly. If the intercessors are ignorant of the offence, their sympathy is necessarily restricted, and likewise they lack the warning and instruction to their souls.

Under the Mosaic law the prescribed course in such circumstances would be the presentation of the sin-offering, according to Leviticus iv., but in a foreign land, remote from the temple and altar of God, this was impossible, and is not named. Neither is any mention made of the peace-speaking blood of Jesus, the way specially opened for the sinner to approach and find mercy. Had James been addressing believers in Jesus he could not fail to present him as the perfect plea for the guilty and the distressed; his blood cleanses from all sin.

As it here stands, the righteousness of human intercessors is the foundation of the hope of pardon and cure: "the fervent prayer of a righteous man prevaileth much." This is so consonant with the hopes and practice of Israel as to give a still more clear impress of these instructions. With that nation the righteousness of certain of their ancestors is their perpetual plea. In Ezek. xiv. 14–20, allusion is made to this hope. And notwithstanding Nehemiah, in his humble confession (chap. ix.), utterly renounces such a plea; and likewise Daniel in chap. ix., yet this is the basis of public petitions presented by the Jews to this very day. So closely does the idea mingle itself with the human heart, that, though we are well aware that we are all sinners, acceptable only in God's beloved Son, yet even we can hardly divest ourselves of the fond persuasion that the prayers of certain distinguished individuals are more efficacious than our own.

In our case, were admission allowed to such an idea

it would tend directly to the disparagement of Jesus as the sinner's only hope. But in regard to Israel we find it repeatedly admitted as a fact. (Ps. xxxiv. 17) "The righteous (plural) cry, and the Lord heareth, and delivereth them out of all their troubles." (Ps. cxlvi. 8) "The Lord loveth the righteous" (plural). (Prov. x. 24) "The desire of a righteous *man* shall be granted." (xv. 2) "The prayers of the upright (plural) is his delight." (xv. 29) "He heareth the prayer of the righteous" (plural).

It would not be suitable here to enter at large into the reasons for this distinction. It may be sufficient to notice that Lev. xviii. 5, explained by Rom. x. 3-5, shows that the footing, on which God proposed to Israel that they should stand, was their own personal righteousness. And that though they, as well as the Gentiles, all failed and "came short of the glory of God;" yet in these instances, as well as in the general character of his dealings with the nation, he ever sought to encourage any approximation towards right conduct. The same may be said of his treatment of the Gentiles, under the then actings of his grace. See Jer. xviii. 7 and 8; Dan. iv. 27.

"Elias was a man of like passions with us, and in prayer he prayed that it might not rain : and it rained not on the land for three years and six months. And again he prayed, and the heaven gave rain, and the land brought forth her fruit."

As an instance of the efficacy of the prayer of a righteous man, James now adduces the case of Elias, or Elijah. He begins by stating that he was of like passions with ourselves. Though a godly and a very faithful man, he was still a man, and therefore subject to human infirmity. This is a very material point. For, on learning the way his prayers were answered, the lowly heart is tempted to say that God heard his prayers because of his freedom from the infirmities of other men, and that what might be true as regards him could not possibly be granted to another man. Therefore does the Apostle thus describe him, that consciousness of demerit might not deter the soul from asking of God. The remark is further of very great importance in the development of Elijah's history.

But what was the subject of his prayer? Was it for the removal of any of the distresses that have been mentioned? Was it that others might be relieved from calamity? for the pardon of their sins? restoration from illness? or for relief from any national, local, or personal trouble? Nothing of the kind! Was it not for the infliction of innumerable calamities upon his countrymen, by withholding rain, one of the first necessaries of life? Not a word about pardon for their sins! If therefore his prayer for the infliction of miseries on the people was granted, will not God more readily hear your elders when they pray for their removal? Three and a half years afterwards Elijah prayed for a cessation of the famine. Abundance of rain was granted the very day he asked for it! James seems to add, let this be your encouragement!

But in all this we do not find Christian truth or hope displayed. The ideas, allusions, and hopes are still Israelitish. Prayer to the God of Israel is still the prominent feature: no mention being made of the person or work of the Lord Jesus Christ, or of his intercession before God.

"Brethren, if any one of you should wander from the truth and one turn him back, let him know that he who turns back a sinner from the error of his way will save a soul from death, and will conceal a multitude of sins."

At the close of his exhortations James endeavours to give fresh impulse to the brotherly love he has been striving to stir into action. He also speaks with more decision as to the object he has upon his heart, though still with much obscurity, probably from the reasons already named.

Moses had forewarned them (Deut. xiii.) as to those who would afterwards entice them to wander from the truth, and lead them to serve other gods. But now they had fallen into the very opposite of this error. He of whom Moses and the prophets had written had come. Him they would not receive. The Prophet whom God had raised up of their brethren, like unto Moses, had been on earth, but from him they stood aloof. So long as they persisted in their rejection of the Son of God, their ways were not wisdom's ways; not paths of pleasantness and peace, but those of death. Refusing him in whom alone is life, nothing but death eternal lay before them. James has been showing how they might render some service to one another in regard to present things; but the greatest possible manifestation of brotherly love would be to lead each other to the feet of Jesus. Then, and then only would the greatest good be accomplished. The soul of the sinner would then be saved from death; and the multitude of his sins be for ever hidden from God's eye, because of the blood of the Lamb which cleanses from all sin. Safe and happy for ever are they who put their trust in Jesus the Son of God.

In this gracious manner does the Spirit of God, through James, seek to restore the soul of the sinner by inducing in him a desire to restore his brother, as the greatest proof he can give of his affection towards him. If he should succeed in bringing him to Jesus, or if he come himself, he will find in him a friend whose love will not merely cover a multitude of sins, but, in the language of Prov. x. 12, will cover all sins!

CONCLUSION.

Having now gone through the Epistle in detail, it might seem desirable to present an epitome of its contents. Owing, however, to its peculiar character, this cannot be properly done. It is plain that in particular passages certain points are prominently dwelt upon; yet notices of these points are found occurring elsewhere. Containing as it does hints, allusions, and intimations, having a general bearing easy to be understood, but of which the full force and poignancy could be comprehended only by those addressed, it is scarcely to be expected that a satisfactory summary could be given: or if attempted that it could convey anything of the inherent cogency of the epistle. These hints and allusions, moreover, are so interwoven, and so thoroughly permeate the whole, that to attempt a condensation would be only to repeat what has been already written. But it may be admissible to trace certain lines of pervading thought.

The most prominent feature of the epistle is its wholly Israelitish character. Topics, sentiments, allusions, references, have all this stamp. The Law of Moses and its injunctions are the basis of the argument. The condemnation spoken of is for violations of that Law. The encouragements to better courses are drawn from the same Law. The personages introduced, Abraham, Rahab, Elias, are all in connexion with their forefathers. Job, too, though not an Israelite, is so bound up with Old Testament narrative, and God's dealings with him are so typical of Israel's position and their past and future history, that the mention of his name is only an intimation about themselves. It might have been anticipated that the servant of Jesus Christ would have preferred to draw attention to the endurance of his glorious Master, rather than to that of Job; but this under the circumstances was impracticable. Also that the faith and works of Jesus would have been dwelt upon rather than those of Abraham; but this also was not thought advisable in this case; though Paul in writing to the Hebrews (xii. 2–4) takes occasion to exalt him to whom the glory is so due.

So exclusively is the horizon limited by and filled with the Israelite idea, that a foreigner could not point to any passage and say, herein James was decidedly thinking of me. On the contrary, every line intimates a knowledge of the Old Testament Scriptures, such as the Israelite alone could possess, and the bearing of which he alone could appreciate. His intellect alone was furnished with the requisite information. In like manner the heart of the Israelite alone could be affected by appeals exclusively addressed to the nation, and not

CONCLUSION.

to the Gentiles or to the Church. It cannot be maintained that there is in it any direct teaching to the Church of God. Place it by the side of either of Paul's epistles, to the Romans, Corinthians, Galatians, Ephesians, etc., the striking dissimilarity and contrast is at once seen. Truths are contained in both, but they are not the same truths. Exhortations are given in each, but they are by no means identical, nor are they based on the same foundation.

If for instance brotherly love is to be inculcated, James shows that any failure therein is a breach of the Law, and that it leaves the soul in a state of ruin as having broken the whole of the Law. Paul, on the contrary, puts it in this way, "Be ye kind one to another, tender-hearted, forgiving one another, even as God in Christ has forgiven you. Be ye therefore imitators of God, as dear children."

If works are to be advocated, James presents the subject in a manner so analogous to what the Law demanded, and to the hopes and constant effort of Israel, that it might almost be thought he was advocating justification by works; though, as we have seen, this is not really the case. Paul, on the other hand, in Rom. vi., also urges the importance of works; but his plea is, that since you have been united to Christ in death and in resurrection, and are now not under law but under grace, "therefore yield yourselves unto God as those that are alive from the dead, and your members as instruments of righteousness unto God."

In respect to Israel having acquaintance with divine truth as revealed in the Old Testament, it must be remembered that this by no means implied that their hearts were subject to that truth. As in the case of Balaam, his knowledge of the will of God did not prevent his seeking to frustrate that will; or, as in the still more striking case, Jonah's far deeper knowledge of the will of God did not imply that his heart was subject to his voice; so Israel's knowledge did not induce a corresponding subjection of heart to what they knew. Neither did the superior knowledge in the Scribe and Pharisee prevent their giving themselves up to wickedness. In like manner the intelligence of the Twelve Tribes did not prevent them from practising the deeds of darkness.

Works of the flesh, as enumerated in Gal. v. 19-21, seem to have abounded in them : nor is there an intimation of any symptom of uprightness to qualify the dark picture. As to morality none is to be traced. Their faith seems to have been that of the antinomian, producing no other fruit than a crop of nettles. The commands of their God had been entirely set aside. All this proves conclusively that they were in a state of utter ruin, though professing to cleave to God in synagogue attendances.

It is also to be noticed that no mention is made of temple, sacrifice, or priest : nothing about lawyer, scribe, Pharisee, or Sadducee : nothing that connects them with the land of their forefathers. Nor is there any reference to the promises of their restoration, so numerous in the Scriptures. The only ecclesiastical features are the Rabbi and the Synagogue, wherein there appears a marked resemblance to the position of the Jews at the present day.

This disclosure of their ruined condition is not in-

CONCLUSION. 87

tended by the Apostle to cast them down in hopeless despair. To leave them in such a state would not be at all in accordance with the mind of God. He has not finally cast them off. Their privileges are not abrogated; only in abeyance. But so long as they continue to refuse Jesus, no promised blessing can be theirs, either eternal or temporal. The design is to induce them to receive him; but how this is to be brought about? How can people be reached who are so very far off, so much farther off, by reason of their prejudices, than the Gentiles, and so demoralised? Their spiritual state appears far beneath that of the Hebrews, to whom Paul wrote.

If the brightness of the noon-day sun were caused to shine upon those long accustomed to walk in darkness, the eyes would shut more closely. The beams of the Sun of Righteousness would be repugnant to those who hated him. Thoughts of eternal happiness and of heavenly glory would have no attraction to those grovelling in the mire of this world. In the absence of all true religious emotion the mind could only be reached through channels familiar to them, along which hopes had floated down, which they had stretched forth the hand to grasp. Such was the hope of attaining to righteousness by their own effort. But though this hope receded in proportion as the soul was earnest in its endeavour, still the Apostle makes use of it as the only principle that was not dormant, but gave some feeble indications of vitality.

Of the two grand divisions comprising man's righteousness, "Love to God with all the heart, soul, mind, and strength;" and "Loving thy neighbour as thyself," it were vain to make mention of the former. Its elevation was too sublime for man even to contemplate, much less to seek after. The other was considered to be more within reach; and though but a portion, and that an inferior portion of the command, it is in human estimation apt to assume such dimensions as to eclipse the greater. In the narrative of the rich young ruler, (Matt. xix. 16, etc.,) it may be observed that our Lord does not test him at all on the First Table of the Commandments; only on the Second; and under this test his righteousness is found defective. The reason I apprehend is, that man's moral perceptions seldom rise above what he thinks is due to his fellow man, or what is incumbent on him in his neighbour's estimation; fondly persuading himself that if he can but make some approach to what is duty in regard to man, he is very far advanced in his duty to God. The stress of the young ruler's effort is on this point, and the amount of his progress was capable of being ascertained by the simple test, " Go sell that thou hast and give to the poor." As if our Lord had reasoned thus, If thou lovest thy brother as thyself, why shouldest thou have more than he; place thyself on the same footing, and then it will be evident that thou hast as much love for him as for thyself.

James was one of those who had been present on this occasion, and was well aware that it is not by works of righteousness that men are saved, but by the mercy of God in Christ Jesus. Nevertheless he employs this, the purport of the Second Table, both as a touchstone to exhibit to themselves the state of their souls; and also as a lever to rouse the inert soul into activity, not only as regards one another, but to give it the special direction on which he was intent.

"Thou shalt love thy neighbour as thyself" is a principle named in the second chapter, but found to pervade the whole epistle. It gives tone to verses 19–21 of chapter i., and also to verse 27. It governs the first half of chapter ii., and underlies the latter half: its force throughout chapters iii. and iv. is manifest. It is also self-evident throughout chapter v., and culminates in the last two verses. Sometimes as a touchstone it shows up the actual state of things arising from disregard of the precept. Sometimes it shows what ought to be done, or what would be the result if it were righteously obeyed. And sometimes it is used for the purpose of restoring the heart from its estrangement from one another, and more especially from Jesus, the Just One, unjustly condemned, but still their friend.

But this last, the point of greatest importance, all absorbing in its magnitude, is brought forward with extreme circumspection, scarcely more than intimated, so as to obviate all occasion for offence, while there is sufficient distinctness to indicate the design. Anything more definite would have precluded the admission to the homes of Israel even of this measure of the truth, so necessary to their salvation.

When James denounces the oppressor he strikes a chord that vibrates through the heart of the poor. In the midst of their sufferings it is no small consolation to hear that their miseries are not unheeded, and that those who trouble them will be punished for it. The Psalms having in them so much of this nature, commend themselves specially to the afflicted and oppressed.

In chapter iii., the Rabbis, claiming superiority of wisdom, and exhibiting it in mutual jealousies, pride, anger, and violence of language, would, with James's help, make it evident to the people that their wisdom was not from above, whatever the assumption might be. All that they would hear of Jesus would be in full and absolute contrast with the practices of their teachers. If they would but listen to him they would discern heavenly wisdom and its actings, exemplified in the conduct of the great Peacemaker, who in all his ways was both peaceable and peaceloving; and in whom the fruit of righteousness displayed itself so abundantly to the glory and joy of God and the well-being of man.

An Israelite, converted to Jesus as the Christ, would at once set us right as to the object of this epistle, by saying, "It was intended for me in the condition in which I was, not in that in which I am. The desire of the writer was to lead me out of the one state into the other. He could not give full utterance to his wishes by reason of the frame of mind of my fellow countrymen. Nursed in holy zeal for the law; zealous of the traditions of our fathers; partaking of the national hatred against Jesus; would they not with indignation have rejected a letter from one of his followers if it had set forth his claims as Lord and Christ? Here then is a reason for the absence of Christian instruction, and for the presence of much that we should not expect to find in a public letter of a servant of Christ.

James is not one to speak peace where there is no

peace. He does not plaster the wall with untempered mortar. He does not attempt to gloss over the ruinous state of things. Like a prophet of old he denounces boldly their evil ways, yet with tenderness and goodwill. He cannot comfort them, seeing they will not accept Him who is "the consolation of Israel." But at the same time he points to the prediction announcing the appearing of Him who is to raise up the tribes of Jacob and restore the outcasts of Israel.

If the believer in the Lord Jesus Christ finds in the epistle of James little to comfort him, little to elevate his soul, or encourage him to look beyond earth to the glory awaiting him above, let him remember that he is taking up a letter addressed to another, not to himself; a letter which, though replete with instruction to those outside, is not intended for those within the pale of salvation; a letter moreover which is not adapted to the state of mind and heart of any others than those born and brought up in the faith and hope of the House of Israel. It is not intended hereby that this epistle is devoid of utility to him. He may profit largely by it and by every word that God has been pleased at any time to speak to his people of Israel; but if he hopes to benefit in the way his God intends, it can only be by keeping alive in his mind the fact that Moses is not Christ; that the Law was by Moses, grace and truth by Jesus Christ. Moses was a servant in the house; Christ a Son, over his house. It was the Son that brought life and incorruption to light through the gospel, thereby setting aside the Law, " taking it out of the way; nailing it to his cross." Would the child of God, whose privilege it is to know and rejoice in the liberty wherewith Christ has made him free, prefer the condition of a slave, fettered in a dungeon? Would he not rather exult in his emancipation, bask in the sunshine of God's love, and be ever praising him who has redeemed him with his own blood? making it his effort to purify himself even as he is pure; not in order that he may be pardoned, but because he has already received the gifts of pardon and life in Christ Jesus! Would he prefer the food supplied to the prisoner in the dungeon to the rich banquet spread for him by a Father's love in and through the broken body and shed blood of the Lord Jesus?· Surely this would be the act of an insane person, or of one unconscious of what he was doing!

The child of God who really desires to grow in the knowledge and love of God in Christ will find the food he requires, where his Father has amply supplied it, in the writings of Paul, Peter, and John. It is there the rich treasures of a Father's heart are opened up· This is solid diet, feeding on which, he grows out of babyhood into manhood. It is there he will find every direction for his guidance. It is there especially he will learn both to make use of all in his own person, as well as to minister thereby life, health, and vigour to others. Yet we must not forget that "all Scripture is given by inspiration of God, and is profitable for doctrine, for reproof, for correction, and instruction in righteousness : that the Man of God may be perfect, thoroughly furnished unto all good works."

www.ingramcontent.com/pod-product-compliance
Lightning Source LLC
Chambersburg PA
CBHW020157170426
43199CBV00010B/1077